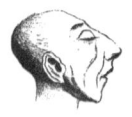 **The Flexible Persona**

Spring 2016 | Vol. 01, No. 01

the Shadows *Issue*

Submissions: *The Flexible Persona* accepts rolling submissions through-out the year via Submittable.com for fiction, creative nonfiction and poetry. See www.theflexiblepersona.com for guidelines.

Upcoming: Fall 2016 issue will be published in August.

Issues: All issues are available for purchase at Amazon.com, Amazon.ca and Amazon.com European affiliates (Amazon.co.uk, Amazon.de, Amazon.fr., etc.).

ISBN-13: 978-0692644997 (The Flexible Persona)
ISBN-10: 0692644997

ISSN [Forthcoming]

Published in the United States by The Flexible Persona.

To learn more about *The Flexible Persona*, visit
www.theflexiblepersona.com.

the Shadows Issue

Word, in fact, becomes a sort of a primary force, in which all being and doing originiate.

– Ernst Cassirer | *Language and Myth*

... our ancestors, forced to live in dark rooms, presently came to discover beauty in shadows, ultimately to guide shadows towards beauty's ends.

– Jun'ichirō Tanizaki | *In Praise of Shadows*

It was strange to be inside myself, walking steadily and rigidly past the fence, putting my feet down strongly but without haste that they might have noticed, to be inside and know that they were looking at me ...

– Shirley Jackson | *We Have Always Lived in the Castle*

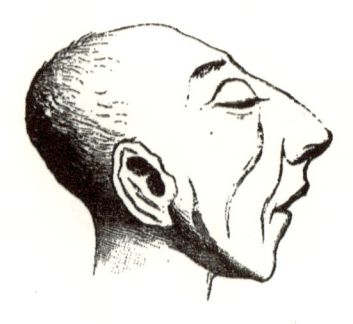

SHADOWS

CONTENTS | SPRING 2016

* *An early draft of this story was awarded a commendation from the* Highlife Highland Neil Gunn Awards.

Introduction

SHADOWS, IN THEIR MOST LITERAL FORM, REMIND US OF THE limits of our sight, our perception. As children, we stay up late in our beds staring at these dark places of our rooms. We project misunderstood monsters and magical lands into these dark spaces, but with maturity and reason the shadows only grow. The Jungians spent a great deal of time wrestling with these larger shadows, the metaphorical shadows, both collective and individual. Those conversations dwell mostly on our repressed evil and sublimated flaws.

Marie-Louise von Franz cautioned against this emphasis, reminding her readers that for Jung himself, the shadow was the whole of the unconscious.[1] It is that layer of mind that, hidden from us, absorbs the world from behind our backs. Exploring the shadows, the unconscious is the most pressing work of the writer. As Robert Olen Butler encourages writers, "... you have to go in there; down into the deepest part of it, and you can't flinch, can't walk away."[2] To delve into the darkness and bring back meaning, that is the alchemy of the word. ●

– Alexander B. Hogan and *Cheska Avery Lynn*

Editors

---

1 Franz, Marie-Louise von. *Shadow and Evil in Fairy Tales.*
　　Revised Edition. Boston: Shambhala Publications, Inc. 1995.
　　Print.
2 Butler, Robert Olen. *From Where You Dream: The Process of*
　　Writing Fiction. Ed. Janet Burroway. New York: Grove
　　Press. 2005. Print.

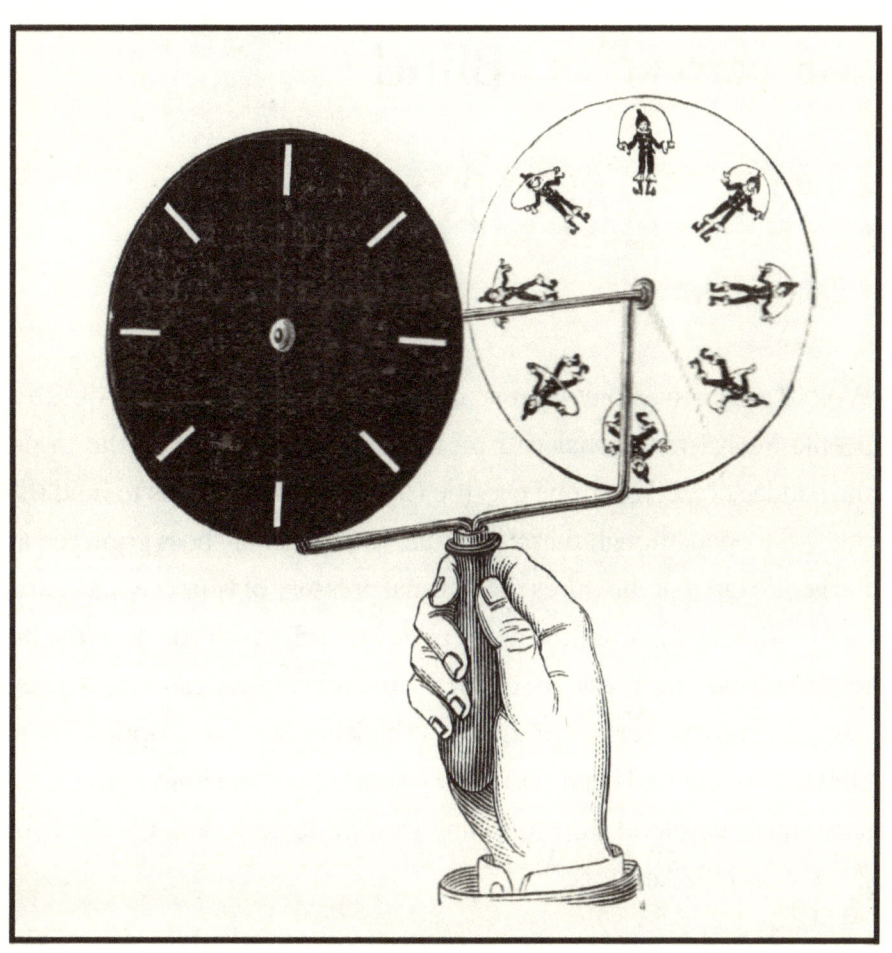

Blind

by Cris Harris

WHEN I TELL THE STORY, IT'S USUALLY THE SMELL THAT FINALLY GETS TO people. Most listeners stick with me through the preliminaries, the drops, the bandage taped over one eye, the *Clockwork Orange* clips to hold the other eye open, though that usually gets a twinge. My boss grimaced at the gentle tap that measures the internal pressure of your eye, and started to withdraw his attention at the pressure cuff, which equalizes the internal and external pressure so that the microkeratome can slice an even 3mm flap into the surface of the eye. I think it was my description of the blinking red light I'd been told to stay focused on, and how, as the pressure equalizes, blood stops reaching your optic nerve and the red light fades away into darkness.

"I couldn't help thinking, this is the last thing I'll ever see, when that light turned to burgundy and then to deep purple and then to black." He was holding his hands up involuntarily at this point, and turning away, looking composed on the outside but internally yelling "La lalalalala I can't hear you." I could tell this by the way he kept tugging at his beard.

But most stay interested through the whir of the microkeratome—which doesn't hurt, and the return of the light, and the bizarre moment when the surgeon delicately, with a tiny tweezers held in his unshaking hand, lifts the flap and opens your cornea to the outside air. The world solarizes, turns metallic and grainy and fuzzy. The surgeon says several times, as his hands grip your head tight as a barber shaving your sideburns with a straight razor, "keep looking at the light," and then the laser pulses come with a cracking sound, like a Geiger counter in an old sci-fi movie. But the kicker, the clincher, the detail impossible to reconcile, the one worse than the replacement of the flap, or the lurching of the motorized, computer controlled table you lie on as it tracks with the laser to ensure proper aim, more memorable than the placement of the foggy bandage lens, worse even than the moment they start in on your remaining eye, is the smoke. The smoke tops it, because you're not even sure you're seeing it, as your cornea is being shaved down to match the version the instruments say will correct all that is wrong with your ability to focus the proper image on the back of your eye. But you can smell the unmistakable aroma of burning hair, wafting over your face, which if you could see it, is lit by the pulsing red beams blinding you while they make you see. You are smelling all that's wrong in your eye burning away. Usually, that's the detail that makes people turn away and not want to hear any more.

As a child, I dreamed of being blind, and it wasn't a nightmare. I idealized the blind characters of my youth, or had them idealized for me. There was Daredevil, blinded by accidental exposure to a radioactive isotope which also heightened all his other sensory powers, gave him a radar sense, and apparently, set him on the course to becoming a lawyer. There was Laura Ingalls Wilder's sister Mary, as played by Melissa Sue Anderson, whose slightly bitchy, prissy, blonde self became noble, vulnerable, and possessed of an unbreakable strength once scarlet fever robbed her of her visual world. I'm not sure if it worked out the same in the books, which I couldn't read, being a boy, but on TV the effect was clear. There were blind Chinese martial arts masters who, paradoxically, "saw" what escaped everyone else, the tragic heroine of *I never promised you a rose garden*, Ben Grimm's blind girlfriend Alicia who not only tamed the love of the Thing but was also hot enough to be constantly preyed on by world-ending super villains who found her exotic enough to stalk. I read biographies of Helen Keller, learned every word of every song in *Tommy*, and was obsessed by an illustrated life story of Braille, though now I only remember two details of his life:

> 1) He blinded himself as a young child trying to punch a hole through a piece of leather with an awl, the leather held before his face so he could see what he was doing as he pushed the awl through from the other side. I could always vividly imagine the strain, the resistance he felt as the tip of the awl raised a little nipple in the leather before punching through and entering his eye. It stuck so deep in his optic nerve that the other eye went dead a few days later.

> 2) The transfiguring moment when, having become a devout Christian at the parochial school for the blind where he ended up, he ran his hands over the open gospel displayed in the chapel, and found he could make out the illuminated letters of the text. This moment in my book was accompanied by a full page illustration of the boy with his hand glued to the Word like someone

The Flexible Persona

grasping an electrical wire, his unseeing eyes wide, jaw dropped in intellectual and spiritual awe, light emanating from his rendered figure to cast the lectern and the altar behind him into sharp relief.

Even the ordinary actual blind people I knew or saw on the bus seemed to have a composure, an apartness that did not invite pity, but rather awe. They could do so much without their eyes that I had trouble doing with mine, or so it seemed anyway. They received special honors, chief among these the right to take their dogs everywhere, tap at the eminently tappable world with a white cane, and like the blind parishioner Ralph at church, be escorted, arm in arm, up the aisle to the communion rail, and back down to his pew by a procession of children like me who competed for the honor.

I dreamed of being blind, and tied bandages over my eyes for hours at a time. I spent whole afternoons learning to navigate my house, armed with a relatively straight branch off the walnut tree. A child who could not sustain attention to any drawing project, building block challenge, or erector set dream creation, I could devote an hour to handling, blindfolded, the objects on the mantle, studying their tangible mysteries in silence and darkness, unlocking the secrets of my father's recorder, the soft silver pitcher (which I once dented with the pressure of my fingertips because I knew I could) the glass paperweight, the surface of the strange blue grey abstract painting that hung there. I left the house sometimes and wandered through the backyard, the garage, even finding my way, blindfolded, painstakingly, up the embankment to the neighbor's fence, up the fence till I could hold the top rail, over to the garage's gutter I could find by waving around my right foot, and, on all fours, the gravel of the shingles rough under my palms, up to the peak of the garage roof, where I sat, not seeing the four yards around us, the waving branches of the trees, the pavement of the driveway below.

My teachers found me out in third grade. I had changed schools, starting at an elite private school that, among other things I had to get used to, required me to learn italic printing. I couldn't get it, and my teacher, Mrs. Nolte, would lose her coiffed, made up calm when I turned in my page of Qs that represented my guess as to what the letter should look like. The other kids had started learning this alphabet in kindergarten, and I was embarrassed into stunned sullenness every time I failed so visibly to make progress. I was, at that time, trying to learn not to wipe my nose on my green uniform sweater, but in these moments, standing before her desk with my substandard letters, I'd fall back to the habit that left what looked like snail trails over my cuffs, and her cheeks would redden under the matte of her base coat. If she got really worked up, you'd see cracks appear.

"Honestly. Look at the chart! What are you thinking! I've told you before, if you don't know the letter, look it up! What's wrong with you?"

"Sorry. I keep forgetting. I'll try again." I smiled sheepishly and tried to edge away but she wouldn't have any of it. If I could just stall a little, I could get someone to show me a good Q and I could learn to copy it. That's what I should have done from the start, but I didn't have many friends yet, nor would I for several years, as it turned out.

"Sorry won't do it. You. Right here. Now look at the capital Q on the chart and write me one right here. Let's go, mister."

I considered my options. I could disobey and push the moment to its crisis, a strategy which might result in having to copy down a dictionary page, with all entries, symbols and minutia—a task which I couldn't actually ever complete, because it had to be in italics, which I didn't know yet, and so I would have to keep at the page, copying and recopying, guessing at the letters I didn't know, until she decided I'd missed enough recesses and wanted me out of her hair. The last time, when I'd blacked the eye of Kristen Ramsey, the daughter of a prominent judge, this had taken three days. Or, I could admit that I didn't know what chart she was talking about.

I looked all around the room, but from where I was I couldn't see an alphabet chart, just a "Who Reads" poster with a perky, mortarboard-wearing cartoon owl atop a stack of books, a display of student artwork (my spaceship sketches not among the selections posted), a blurry times-table chart that came in handy for those sitting right next to it, etc. Members of the class were looking up to the front of the room, some with evident pleasure at seeing the new kid get it again. I didn't know what to say: if I pretended to see the chart, what then? "Oh, right, the chart. Don't know why I keep forgetting to look at that. Great, I'll just go back to my seat then..." I could see how that would play out. Asking for a clue also seemed out of the question. I stood there, and snuffled, and wiped my nose, and a smile broke out across her face. It was a smile of triumph as she figured me out, and it was without kindness.

"You can't see it, can you? You're squinting and you still can't see it! Why, you need glasses!"

"Four eyes," the class clown stage-whispered, and she was off to reprimand him. Allison, who was brainy and occasionally nice to me, pointed up toward the corner where the wall met the ceiling.

"Up there. Around the room."

I put the tips of my index fingers and my thumbs together to make a small diamond shaped hole, raised it to my eye and narrowed it almost to darkness—a trick I'd learned trying to read the announced hymns in church so I could mark each one with a separate ribbon in my hymnbook and be ready to sing without that tiresome shuffling and paging. If I pushed hard, I could read the numbers posted all the way across the church, could even see my father, the priest singing up by the altar. When I tried it this time, the muddy yellow banner that encircled the room right at the top of the wall resolved into an unfurled, parchment-colored strip of paper, about a foot high, striped with two solid lines and a third dotted one. Allison wasn't lying; the alphabet was printed, or at least italicized there, in delicate sepia script. Within the hour, Mrs. Nolte had me in the nurses office, with her cruel pyramid of shrinking, stylized Ns, Zs, Os, Cs, As, and mostly Es. I've hated those charts ever since. I'm stumbling through my forties, eligible (in terms of age) for the presidency of the United States, but at my last eye exam, I felt the old shame and resentment rising up, as I guessed wildly at Ks and Rs, debated the merits of One? or Two? Three? or Four?, admitting that I couldn't see much difference. There must be a rule against encouragement in these situations, because I ask for it but never receive, never have received the least bit of it.

When I got my glasses in early October of 1979, the first thing I noticed was not the leaves on the trees, it was the edges of the buildings. Driving home across the Morrison Bridge, I looked back at downtown Portland and trembled in fear. The buildings were impossibly clear, their edges sharp and towering. How could they stand up? I looked away, afraid to see them come tumbling down, and sad already, to see the comforting cloudy figures of their former looming selves transformed into monoliths, distinct and knifelike. It was the same in my classroom. I still remember how it looked before I got my glasses; warm, fuzzy, a mix of yellows and browns and greens. When I looked around with my newly four-eyed face for the first time, my head hurt at all the specifics of posters and light switches and coats hanging on hooks, the spines of three hundred workbooks, all the writing on the board, and that damned banner encircling the whole room. It was as plain as the blackheads on the nose on my face, and it wasn't a nice creamy off white, it was more khaki, grimy looking somehow. How could I have missed it before? Later that day, I learned why the kids with glasses were so bad at dodge ball—which we called "bounce bombardment" or "bouncemen" for short. When the iconic red rubber ball smacks your face, it drives the glasses into your eyebrows, cheeks and the evermore-sensitive bridge of your nose. If they get you hard enough, the frames can crack, though more often they fall off and the lenses get scratched or shattered when they hit the pavement. After a few rounds, you get hesitant, fearful, and a stink of doom comes off you that every strong-armed kid with a ball can smell. It's enough to drive a child to foursquare.

And yet I looked forward to blindness, imagined my deteriorating vision would somehow make me noble or enviable. Having climbed high in a tree, or wandered lonely to some corner of the playground, I stared at the sun until tears ran down my cheeks. I paid attention to the warning that reading under low light or sitting within inches of the television screen could rob me of the light, and so I turned down lights to read and sat so close to the screen I couldn't see what was happening at the edges. Sure enough, my eyes grew worse and worse. I didn't tell anyone; I was saving it up, all the pity and sorrow and guilt no one seemed to be feeling on my account.

At church, I'd gotten good at staking out the Ralph territory, and made sure I was on hand to seat him, to sit with him, to offer him my skinny arm when we made our way up the aisle. I'd tilt my arm up to indicate through the pressure that we were about to step up, and Ralph would raise his foot for the stair, believing me without hesitation. I led him to the communion rail, where he stared straight ahead, listening for the approaching celebrant, my father and Deacon Thompson. One would place the host on his upturned palm, and the other bring the cup, saying, "the blood of Christ, right in front of you, Ralph," as they held the chalice out so he could guide it to his lips, "the cup of salvation." Ralph was in his late sixties I guessed, stout, bald, red-faced, dandruff flaking the shoulders of the tweed jacket he wore in winter. He had a seersucker suit he wore to weddings which made him look quite dapper. Like all blind people, he never looked you in the eye, but always looked in your direction and smiled. He nodded steadily at the world, as if to say "Uhuh, like I thought, yes sir, well I'll be." Approaching Ralph, you knew you were outside the circle of his awareness until, all at once, you were in his range, and he recognized your voice, or asked "Who's that?" if he didn't. Either way he'd affirm your presence with a nod, as if he'd expected you and you'd just confirmed his expectations, and he was happy about it. He smiled for every meeting and thanked everyone, and shook your hand at the passing of the peace with a palsied grip. His eyes were watery blue, and crinkled at the corners in a kindly way. His watch had a brass cover that flipped open, and no glass over the hands. Sitting beside him, I'd watch him recite his prayers, warble through his hymns, kneel and stand just a hair behind the crowd. Sometimes I'd shut my eyes for long periods to see the service as he did. Sometimes, during the readings, he'd lean down and ask me what the reader had said. If I knew, I'd whisper in his ear, and he'd nod seven or eight times to show he understood.

As I hit middle school, I started going to the eight o'clock service once in a while, where there was no music. I missed the singing, but liked the monastic, spare, solemn quality of it. Even the sermon seemed starker, severe, probably because in those days my father was still hung over in the morning. Or, after he went through rehab and quit drinking, he hadn't yet toked himself into a rapturous marijuana daze at 8:00, but would be feeling no pain by 10:00. Those 10:00 service sermons started to get awfully rambling and disorganized. But the real attraction, of course, was getting to go home early, when everyone else was at church. I could make sickeningly sweet eggnog in the blender, or eat half a loaf of toast while watching TV. I got the funnies all to myself and could play the stereo at full volume. Sometimes Ralph showed up at eight o'clock service too, though I assume for different reasons. It was at one of these quieter, more restrained and poorer attended masses that I realized Ralph didn't actually know all the prayers. He faked it a little, mumbled through sections of the confession, the prayers of the people, and sometimes even began a response at the wrong moment. I started to watch for his head to raise up a little higher than usual and his lips to open, as if he were ready to cast out with his tongue for the missing language like a child trying to catch a snowflake. He knew the refrains of the hymns, but not the verses.

Finally, one coffee hour when I had fetched Ralph some cookies and a paper cup of coffee, I asked him about it. Did he have a prayer book? Or a bible? His face fell, sadder, and more closed than I had ever seen it.

"No, I don't have a bible, though I sometimes get tapes."

"You read Braille don't you, Ralph?"

"Pretty good, I do. But those things, those Braille books are expensive, yes sir. I do ok." He had his smile back, was nodding, but it seemed kind of fake to me, an artificial resignation I recognized as meant to cover up real desire.

My buddy Mike Thompson, the son of the deacon, talked about it with me. What would it take? How much could it cost to get Ralph a Braille bible and prayer book? His dad did the research, and it got very serious. We would need hundreds of dollars. Sts. Peter and Paul was a working class Episcopal church whose population held a lot of "recovering Catholics." It wasn't a blue-blood Anglican fortress of wealth by any means, but we figured it couldn't hurt to ask. The next Sunday we started our sales pitch at coffee hour. It was slow at first. One older man who wore western style shirts with wide stripes loudly proclaimed that I'd not get a damned cent out of him. A sharp-chinned woman with a dead tooth in her grimace asked me how much I'd be putting in? I didn't hesitate.

"$20. I'm saving up from my allowance money and mowing lawns for it," I told her, looking right in her eyes. It wasn't entirely untrue, as I did intend to put some money in. Deacon Thompson had warned us that we would need to pledge some seed money to get it going. After a long pause, she withdrew a thin embroidered wallet from her purse, snapped the clasp open and gave me a ten-dollar bill. She didn't smile, but put her hand on my head and wished me luck.

It took us six weeks to raise the money, which doesn't seem so long now, but at thirteen, was an epic task. The last $150 came from the wife of the man who'd yelled at us the first Sunday. She said it was just to stop us pestering everyone, honestly, but she winked as she handed me the check. We gave all the money to Deacon Thompson, who put in the order, but told us it might take eight to ten weeks for delivery. This is what we told the contributors when they skeptically asked us for a timetable. I got the sense they thought we had cheated them somehow, and I worried that they could see I hadn't actually put my pledge in, because we had raised enough. I had talked myself into a picture of how it would be though, me holding my red prayer book up to read the post-communion prayer I had never memorized, Ralph standing there with his black Braille prayer book (I don't know why I imagined it as black and leather bound, but I did) one finger scanning back and forth across the page while he intoned, his voice grown strong, confident as he read along. I told it that way to impatient investors, who usually grunted and walked away placated, but not all with smiles on their faces. These interactions grew more strained as the delays mounted.

Part of the strain no doubt came from the fact that that spring my father had insisted on coming out as a gay man to the vestry, even though the bishop had told him in no uncertain terms that if he wanted to stay in the active priesthood he needed to keep his homosexuality tightly closeted. But Dad had already come out to the family, had announced his intention to divorce our mother, and seemed set on leaving the priesthood that denied him the privilege of being who he was. He got his wish right away; the vestry removed him from duty as soon as he was done speaking his piece, and he never preached from that pulpit again. My mother and sister kept going to the church, even after we moved across town, but I went with them less frequently. It was awkward, and shameful, and people were often crying over my mom. That was my excuse for not being there the day Deacon Thompson and Mike presented the Braille bible and Book of Common Prayer to Ralph at coffee hour. It came in four file-box sized containers, running to some thirty volumes, a detail I had failed to appreciate when imagining Ralph using the books in church. Mike and his dad had brought the boxes in to the hall before the services, which risked nothing, as Ralph couldn't see them when he walked by. After Mass, Deacon Thompson had called out for everyone to come around for the presentation of a gift. Mike sat Ralph down at a chair, and his dad gave a short speech praising the parishioners for their generosity, and especially thanking Mike and me for working to solicit the donations. My mom said he spoke highly of us, and did not linger on my inability to be there that morning. Then they helped the baffled Ralph open the first box and watched to see his reaction.

In fact, I could have gone to church that day, and wanted to be there to see all the work come true, and in fact I knew in advance that the presentation was to be that day, though my mother did not. I chickened out in part because I hated the idea of embarrassing Ralph, and the idea that he would be obligated to say thank you, and that all the eyes would be on me. I was 13, and liked attention usually, but in this case, just thinking about it made my skin crawl. Here was something I'd done that was actually sort of selfless, a Goody Two-shoes, hey look at me doing good kind of thing that, because we stuck with it, actually turned out and could result in making no one unhappy. It made my stomach hurt to think of being there. I promised to go to the eight o'clock service nearby the rental house we'd moved into, but instead stayed home and watched the clock.

When Ralph opened the box, Mike said, he seemed flustered and even a little angry somehow. Serious. And then he started to say, "Well, I'll be. Well. I'll be" over and over again as he started to run his fingers over the pages. He was out of practice, as it turned out, and it took him a while to figure out what he was reading. And then he wept, the tears running down his cheeks. Mike said he sobbed and blew his nose on his white handkerchief and dripped tears on the off-white pages full of bumps.

I hardly ever went back to that church, and never gave Ralph a chance to thank me. I thought I'd avoided ever seeing Ralph cry until I had to go back to the church to bury my father, who they'd welcomed home at last. Ralph was there, a little more stooped but basically looking the same. He was wearing a seersucker suit, perhaps the same one, crying as he was lead out the door. I've never known his last name.

The first time I ever actually feared going blind was before that, and it should have de-romanticized the whole thing for me, but the effect only lasted a few minutes. My brother and I were home alone, and up to mischief. I don't remember why we were cutting several lengths of electrical cord, but it couldn't have been for noble purposes. Perhaps we were binding something, or perfecting the electronic ignition systems we used to set off homemade bombs, or were planning something spectacular with the neon power supply we used to burn elaborate, carbonized trails across the surfaces of doors, chests of drawers, and cherished books no one looked at very often. My glasses were broken again, and wouldn't stay on my face when I tried to practice with my brother's nun-chucks, or "nunchacku" as he liked to call them. It was 1982. He called me over to the lamp in the living room where he was measuring out the wire, and asked me to hold it tight with both hands while he sawed through it. He was using a Buck lock-back with a six inch blade that he gave me a couple years later when he'd forgotten to purchase a Christmas present. I obliged him, wrapping the ends around my fists and spreading my hands apart as hard as I could. I held my right hand close to my waist, and extended my left about two feet away from me. My brother sat to my right. The wire was insulated and didn't bite into my palms too badly. But even with my help he was still having trouble, and I was having trouble holding the wire up when he pushed down on it. So he switched to sawing from below, so I could put my weight against his cutting force. I wanted to go get my glasses so I could see what he was doing, but figured I could wait. After a few moments struggling and swearing, I leaned down to get the wire within my close vision, my nearsightedness having already grown so severe that I had to hold books up to my nose to read. My face was probably less than a foot from the knife when it came through, too close for Joseph to stop his upward motion. The blade went in my left eye socket, hit bone, and bounced my head back. He screamed, which in some ways, was the scariest part.

I moved quickly, my left hand covering my eye, holding back the pulp I imagined was ready to fall out on the living room rug. I stumbled toward the bathroom mirror. Joseph couldn't follow. He told me later that he was almost sick right there, and was already wailing with regret and horror and shame. I don't remember what was coming out of my mouth, but there was a lot of pain roaring in my ears, and it was wet under my hand. His noise, his teary apologies (for what exactly? It was just as much my fault, when you think of it) receded like the sounds of the surf. I hesitated in front of the mirror and so I have the image firm in my memory, the wire still wrapped around my hand, my right eye open as wide as it could go, my face white with fear, a drop of blood running out from underneath my palm. I pulled it back and I could see the wound, a perfect, half-inch line on my left lower eyelid, dark blood seeping from it, already slowing. It took me a minute to realize I could see it with both eyes. The whole side of my head, deep in my face ached, but I could see. That's how my brother found me, laughing as I wiped the blood away and watched the line of red slowly reform under my eye.

What we figured is that the blade, turned so that its flat ran parallel to the width of my eye, had punched through my eyelid but gone *under* my eyeball, and had hit bone at the back of my eye socket. My vision was teary and pinkish from the little bit of blood in my eye, but the tissues I dabbed with went from dark to red to pink to just damp over the course of ten minutes or so. An enormous bruise formed there, and my left eye just plain hurt for days, but I could see. He and I talk about this particular close call, one of many, periodically. He still gets the chills when he talks about it.

"It's just that it hit so hard," he says, and shakes his head. "I was so sure I'd killed you, just punched into your skull."

"Nope. Dodged it that time," I'll say, and it's not that I'm trying to be brave, it's just that when I remember this incident it's mostly with a rising giggle at my insane good fortune. I grin as I recount with him, a half inch, a quarter inch even and it would have been a different story altogether. As it was, we didn't even tell our parents, though for a while I could threaten him by calling "I'll tell mom you stabbed me in the eye with your knife!" but even these threats paled away. It would have been hard to explain, and soon there was some new secret we were keeping anyway. When I was in college and we did finally tell our mom, she just sighed and looked lost, one more piece of evidence that her sons were doomed, claimed by a violent fate outside her control.

Long term, the first effect, and only one I can definitively attribute to the injury, is that when I used to box, a blow to my left cheek would often split the faint, hairline scar wide open. And over the years, as my vision deteriorated, eventually getting so bad that if I held my glasses at arm's length they disappeared into the ocean of blur out there, so bad I couldn't walk safely on an uneven surface, couldn't see house numbers of highway exits even with my glasses, couldn't pass my van driver physical without some hints from the examiner about line three, my left eye led the way towards darkness. I had a bad eye and a worse eye, an eye so dim it saw colors differently, so warped it saw the perfect full moon as a smear of faint light. But that could have nothing to do with having a knife probe my eye socket all those years before. One eye had to be worse than the other, after all, and though my left eye was the one the surgeon wasn't sure he could correct, in the end, my cornea was thick enough to allow the degree of reshaping they needed.

I've thought of the moment the wire came into focus and the knife flashed up often. Visually, I remember a flash of red, not unlike my visual memories of taking a good right jab in the eye, or what I saw when I once grabbed an electric stock fence, or my associations with falling out of a tree and breaking my left arm. Flashes of red, like a blinding red light masking the whole world. A red curtain drawn swirling over everything, and the sinking feeling that if you can't get it to part in a second or three, or five, it will stay with you forever.

When I got up from the table, half an hour later and $4500 poorer, I had matching flaps cut into both eyes, corneas re-forged by laser pulses, and cloudy bandage lenses serving as the scales that were to fall from my eyes the next day at noon during my one day follow-up. My eyes hurt, and my primary emotion was relief that I had not panicked and tried to sit up while the laser was firing. No, my fear of embarrassment had once again trumped my fear of permanent physical damage, and I had been a good patient, though the bile rose in my throat and I might have chewed some silver slivers loose of my fillings. Sitting up, I expected the fog to be total, and was surprised when the blue capped, blue-bloused, white-sneakered nurse handed me a little faux leather bag with my eye drops, instructions, artificial tears in .01 ml plastic ampules, and my glasses inside. I was surprised because my hand reached out and grabbed it, because through the fog, I could see it. I could see the pattern in the linoleum, the door handle, and as my wife guided me out of the building, the stairs, the tile work, the glass louvers on the front windows. While she drove us east on I90, panel trucks loomed up outside the window, and I read their logos to her. At my appointment the next day, when they pulled the bandage lenses loose, Dr. Wilson, who seemed less interested in me now that I'd paid, declared me 20/30 and legal to drive.

Over the next two weeks, I had to put drops in my eyes four times a day, holding my eyes shut for a full minute after the first, and then waiting four minutes before administering the second. One was an antibiotic and the other a topical anesthetic, but I never figured out which was which. I kept my drops on the windowsill of the guestroom, and four times a day, first thing upon waking, right before lunch, right before dinner, and right before bed, I sat in the bentwood rocker by the window and diligently dropped cloudy and clear solutions in my eyes. During the four minutes between solutions, I stared out the window, every day able to see a little more, a little more clearly.

After the surgery, I wore out the attention spans of family and friends with the details of my recovery and my worries that I wasn't recovering fast enough. Finally, even my doctor responded to my complaints of dry eyes and discomfort by reminding me wryly "We did cut your eyes open, you know." I do know, but can't believe it. I have swum in a mountain lake and seen trout cruise fearlessly away from my shadow, seen the stars as I slept out at night now, have had the pleasure of being able to wash my feet in the shower and see them get clean, have risen from the bed on a summer night and walked, scarred and pierced perhaps, but naked as I was born down the moonlit hall to the bathroom. I have woken to the world as a pattern that can be resolved as soon as I choose to see it as my hand clutching the blanket, the open bedroom doorway, the sparse decoration of the guest room across the hall, window beyond the guestless bed, apple tree swaying in the breeze, hedgerow beyond that, and blue sky peeking through the leaves. It takes only a few blinks and the trick of remembering to see depth without straining past fuzziness, and it leaves me, almost every sunny morning, amazed at my luck.

But there is another side to the gold coin of vision. I gained sight (by six months 20/20 right, 20/25 left), but have lost the ability not to see. In an endless faculty meeting, or tiresome class discussion, I can no longer remove my glasses with studied scholarly concentration, put the temple of my glasses on my lower lip, look thoughtful and make whatever idiot is speaking dissolve into a distant fog. I had a gauzy veil ready for the world, and chose it more often than you might expect, turning a sunset into a Monet, a candlelit face into an airbrushed portrait, my paunchy middle in the mirror a distant and unimportant piece of background. I knew a corrected world and an impressionist universe beyond the lenses, always waiting. I had two ways of seeing, both imperfect, now there's just eyes open and eyes shut. But the surgery, you can't go back from the surgery, and day by day, I forget that other way of groping through the world, that ability to put the limit of vision right at the end of your arm.

It is wrong, I know, to mourn one's own weaknesses, but there are lots of wrongs here. It's wrong to romanticize noble suffering, wrong to see the blind as metaphors, wrong to be party to self-destructive behavior, wrong to do so many things in our histories. Wrong, probably too, to define ourselves by our abilities and by our disabilities, both of which can desert us, leave us with only our pitiful explanations to account for ourselves. But the truth of it is we all finger our scars, dwell lovingly on the reminders of wounds mostly healed. We remember our nightmares with a fondness, almost. We try, at least, to remember how they went. I imagine Lazarus after the big day, reclining at home, lost in thought, staring into space a lot while his loved ones make excuses for him to the company. He closes his eyes, but he can't see the tomb anymore. He smiles sheepishly at his visitors, who can't take their eyes away from his face. He clears his throat to tell a story. •

Xenophobia

by Elena Botts

IT IS LIKE, YOU ARE AT A ROOFTOP PARTY AND EVERYONE—EVEN THE sun— is dancing, undulating through the discarded champagne bottles and two camera lenses, both pointed at you, for the moment at least, the Johannesburg skyline forgotten, a purple Mandela grinning justice across the business district and a little fire escape staircase winding its fine way up 'til heaven, but somewhere down below weaves the subtler masses in their street wear finery and you're thinking of the jackets emblazoned in tribal patterns, this new one you've got at market, and you're thinking of a lot of things, you're thinking of the word "justice" and a people's justice, you're thinking about a lot of things but the word justice doesn't do it justice and you're thinking about a lot of things.

And then it's no longer Sunday sunlit and shimmering strange through the knotted streets and myriad ways of Braamfontein. It's Monday. You're three floors below and four streets away, one across and to the left. The woman is crying. You tell her, please don't cry. She's got a lovely face, such pretty eyes, tight little universes inside. You realize you've said nothing. You're just watching her.

The best thing to say sometimes is, is there anything more you'd like to say? Because then the refugees have a chance to speak, but more than that, they have someone sitting quietly who will listen. And nowhere, in any part of the world, is that a small gift, to be truly heard.

So I listen. But afterwards, I admit, I'm frantic. The persecuted, the assaulted, the escaped and the wanted. I am desperate to assure them of some status in a somewhat stable democratic country. I am desperate to assure them of things I cannot promise so rapidly, so I appeal to all legality and then try my hardest to write them the letters begging asylum because when they thank me in whatever language, I ought to meet their eyes, wherein lies an undying kind of vast human dignity.

And this is not even my work yet. The truth gets farther. My supervisor is interested in xenophobia, which is phantasmal, an invisible force that seems to pull society every which way, a silent demon at its seams. But not really, no, it's more of a quiet voice in every human mind, playing upon our individual fears so singularly placed inside. Until relationships morph and shift—the whole thing, tectonic—and the dynamics of societal interrelationships are entirely different. Until fear shatters these and we shake apart and there's a man with a bloody knife and there is the government standing outside, looking away as—and here's the refugee again, man or woman, someone shipwrecked from nation and just landing, and oh, they all say this—"looking for a safe place"—like the woman who wandered for nine days straight through the wild African forest after being raped by rebel men, just "looking for a safe"—and the gay man who was persecuted everywhere he went in his homophobic country, just "looking for," and the woman whose government was bent on erasing her life to gratify some twisted need for power- "safe place." What an idea, of a safe place, that a stable democracy—and these words carry more weight when unused to, when they are a brief but undocumented dream, sorry I meant unattainable dream, and then to arrive at a place and for it to be safe except that there is a silent demon of xenophobia, but sorry, this is no demon, it is inextricable from the sweet vitality of human-ness, its rotted gracelessness tied in thick to gracefulness, to the divine ingenuity of every human mind, merely rooted and grown in fear, flowering hatred, eventually spawning violence. To arrive in a safe place, and find it not safe? This is far away, it is far away from the word justice, though justice may be another false dream, and far from this one brief human dream, still one might dream. One might, at least, for the sake of compassion, seek to make things, in the stable democracy more opposed to the stealthy unwritten habits of the xenophobe, though not right, closer to the sleeping heart of this human thought, "justice," closer indeed to instilling this "safe place," or love for the refugees, for those who need. •

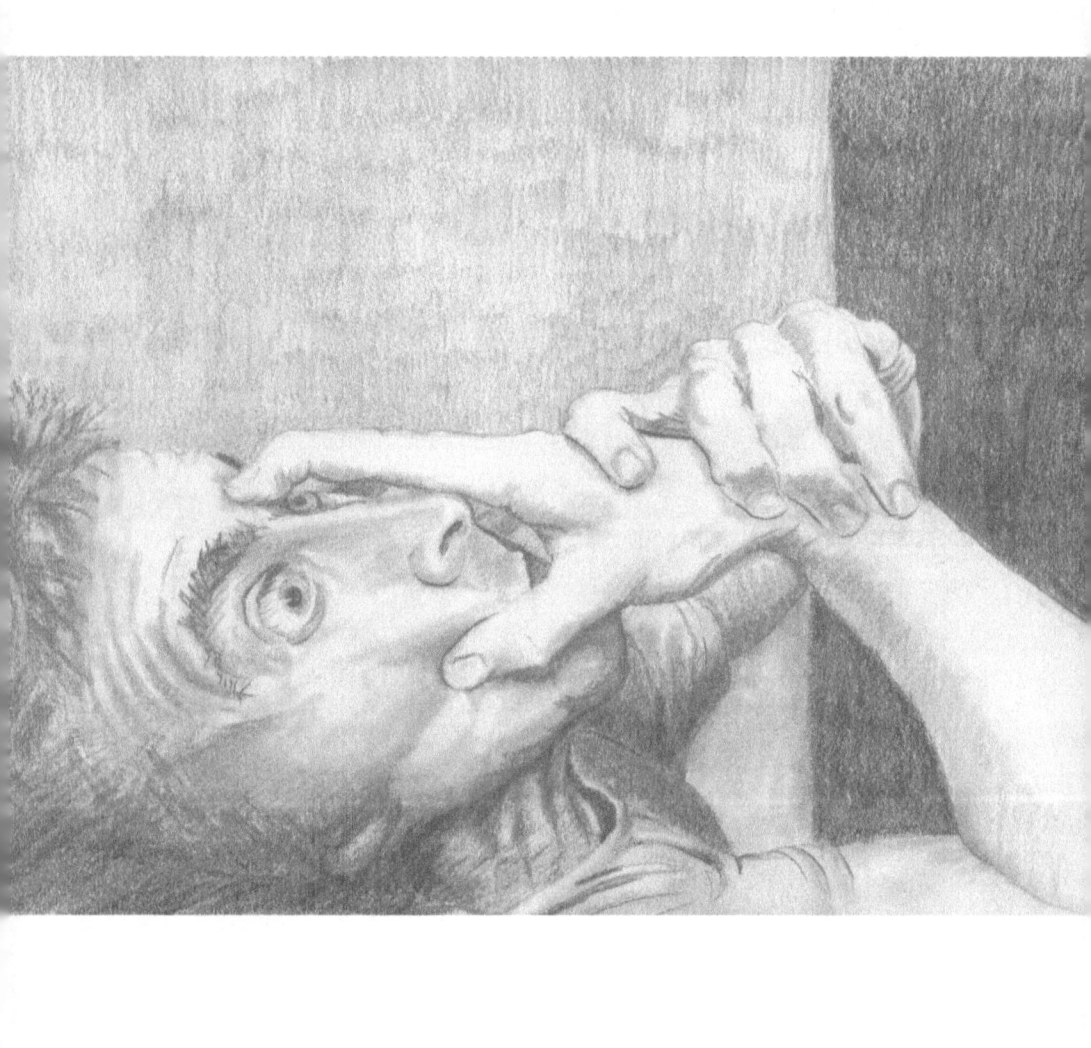

Self-Defence 1, Alisdair Small

FATTIES

by Gael DeRoane

EVERYBODY AROUND HERE IS FAT. I GO TO THE GROCERY STORE AND IT'S ALL fat people. Fatties browsing the cookie aisle, pulling tubs of ice cream off the freezer shelves, crowding around the old lady holding a free-sample tray of sausage morsels or some other processed crap. And it's not just the customers. Most of the cashiers are fat, too. Even some of the stock boys, I notice, have love handles spilling over their belts. Except how can you call them love handles when there's nobody who wants to love *or* handle them? Trust me, these stock boys aren't getting any.

People driving their cars in the oncoming lane, you can see their fat faces when they pass by. One of the tellers at the bank I go to has peanut butter cups in a glass jar on a shelf next to her chair. Her hand is fat like a baby's hand. This teller, her name is June, always gives me a big smile, and I appreciate the effort because I'll bet there's no real happiness behind that smile. Spend some time with fat people and you'll find out pretty quick that they're anything but jolly.

My mom, for example, who isn't even the fattest hog in the pen, is totally miserable. She has a round face with a double chin and blubber at the waist, but she can get in and out of a car without too much trouble, and her legs are actually kind of attractive. One night when she was feeling sorry for herself, I said at least be glad you don't have cankles. I had come in early for me—around nine or so—and I knew she was down in the dumps because she was sitting on the couch eating cake and ice cream out of this huge mixing bowl. That's her favorite comfort food, what she shoves into her face after a dating tragedy or a problem at work. I plopped down in the Lazy-Boy that dad used to sit in before he left, and I watched a few minutes of some lawyer show with her. I got bored after a while and started talking, and that's when I mentioned the cankles thing. She didn't know what cankles were, so I told her they were fat calves that went straight down to the ankles like a big log of bologna, and I reminded her that she was not afflicted with such a mutation. But she took it the wrong way. What the fuck, man, *she* was the one who brought up the subject of being fat, saying that someone should kill her for eating all that cake and ice cream. But when she's in that kind of self-pitying mood it doesn't matter what I say. I can't win. You're skinny now, she said, her voice getting shrill, but just wait a few years. Wait till your metabolism changes, you'll be big as a house.

That is *so* not happening.

*

If you think I don't like fat people, you'd be wrong. I feel sorry for them. Everybody—except for models and movie stars, I guess—hates *something* about the way they look. But fat people hate their whole bodies, and that must be awful. I hate my feet. I've got that second toe thing, how it sticks out in front of all the other toes. I envy Claire, my best friend, who has perfect little toes all in a row. She paints the nails orange or blue and walks around in flip-flops, showing them off. Eric, my boyfriend, hates that he's already going bald at thirty. One day we were sitting in Wegman's parking lot and this incredible fat guy walked in front of the car. He must have been four hundred pounds. His clothes—a blue T-shirt and khaki pants—could have fit a baby elephant. He was wearing some kind of boots that he couldn't even close because his feet were so fat. Eric and I watched in silence as he lumbered to his car, carrying two plastic bags probably filled with donuts and cookies. He was a mess, disgusting, but you couldn't help noticing that he had this mane of thick, luxuriant hair.

Eric said, Jesus, look at his hair. Some guys have all the luck.

I just laughed. I've grown tired of telling Eric that his balding skull doesn't bother me. Looks don't matter to me that much, really. While we were watching the fat guy walk away I told Eric that even if he looked like Quasimodo I'd still do him, because I like his mind. Thanks a shit-load, he said, and of course I realized it was the wrong thing to say to a guy who's bummed about his appearance.

I've been with Eric for almost a year, but I don't see much future in it. He can sense that I'm ready to walk, so lately he's been picking on me. Like about the way I dress. I'm a retro-hippie, tie-dyed and hempy. He dresses like a biker with Goth overtones, though I don't believe he's ever straddled anything more powerful than a Schwinn. I have a *Save the Whales* T-shirt that he made fun of. What's so special about whales, he said. Why not *Save the Planaria*? I didn't know what a planaria was, and he made fun of me for *that*, too. When he told me they were a kind of worm I said big deal, you were a bio major so you know all that useless crap. Lot of good it's doing him, too, now that he works for the university's computer center.

That's a mistake I don't plan on making. I'm a psych major, and I want to be a social worker. I don't care about the shitty pay and the lack of esteem. I want to help people, because I have a compassionate Buddha heart beating under my ribs, and fuck Eric or anyone else who wants to make fun of that.

*

I liked Buddha the first time I ever heard about him. I liked that he sat under a tree waiting for enlightenment to come to *him*. Sort of like Newton with the apple. I've never been big on striving. My dad, who's this nauseating go-getter type (his hero was Pete Rose, which tells you everything you need to know about him), used to yell at me for bad report cards. What the hell's wrong with you, he'd ask. Why can't you study more? It's hard, I would say, when you have the work ethic of Marie Antoinette.

I learned about Buddha in Professor Kantrowitz's American Lit class. We were doing the Beats, and he told us how Kerouac and Ginsberg and those guys studied Buddhism. Dr. Kantrowitz—but I call him Sid now, because we fucked—was very eloquent when he described how Buddha ran out on his wife and baby one night, and left a note explaining that just because birds sit together on a branch for a little while, it doesn't mean they'll stay there forever. Sid had just dumped his wife, so I guess that part of the story really got to him. One night at Sid's apartment I found a picture of the wife when I was rummaging through his stuff while he was in the bathroom. Fat and fifty. Sid's past fifty, too, but he's not fat. Just short and homely, in an appealing, *Woody Allenish* way.

Lest you think I have some kind of mental problem that prevents me from hooking up with anyone hot, I will tell you that my boyfriend before Eric was a dead ringer for Colin Farrell. He didn't dump me, either. We just sort of came apart, no big deal. I do lots of guys, and I don't see anything wrong with it. It's an interesting lifestyle.

Better put that in the past tense. After Sid I'm not so sure I'll be fucking somebody just because I'm horny and he's a little bit interesting. You'd think a guy who's lived as long as Sid would be smart about life, but one night after just a couple of months of us being together he said maybe we should get married. No way that was happening, and I told him as much. It was a bad idea to give him the news while I was still naked. He couldn't handle the derailment. He started raging around the apartment, throwing his hands in the air and saying I'd ruined his marriage and his life, which wasn't fair because he'd shitcanned the wife before we even got started. I tried to calm him down while putting my clothes on. It was a very awkward scene. Finally I just told him he was being an asshole and hoisted my backpack and headed for the door. I turned to say goodbye for the last time. He stared at me, an anguished look in his watery old eyes. You have the face of an angel, he said, but the heart of Dr. Mengele. I knew the gravity of the insult because I'd recently seen Gregory Peck as this Dr. Mengele dude in *The Boys from Brazil*. Okay, if that's what he thought of me I wouldn't spoil the picture. I'm glad you think I'm pretty, I said, and walked out of his life forever. Not very compassionate, I know.

But he asked for it.

*

Since Eric and I are not officially splittsville yet, you might think that my dalliance with Sid was cheating, but I would disagree. I know for a fact that Eric has been boning this mousy twat he works with and also that he's picked up a bar slut or two while we've been together. No problemo. Our contract is not exclusive. Still, I imagine the time will come when it gets too pissy or weird and we have this ludicrous dramatic breakup, which will be unfortunate because I like hanging with him.

The thing is, I'm growing tired of sex. I asked Claire if she thought it was possible to be burned out sexually at the tender age of twenty. We were polishing off our chocolate shakes at Five Guys, and she almost did a spit take. We're pigs, she said. We're just getting started.

I'm not so sure. I foresee a period of celibacy coming into my life, although I'm wondering does that mean I can't use my pocket rocket once in a while. I mean, I can't imagine never being turned on again. But what I *don't* want is the mess and entanglement that comes with getting your rocks off with a guy. I can handle it myself, thank you.

I want to be a real Buddhist. I want to separate myself from all things that will cause me to suffer because I desire them. And that includes guys who turn out to be creepy when that's the last thing you expect them to be. Like last week when I bumped into Andy Whalen at the mall. I was in Hot Topic checking out T-shirts with rude sayings on them, and there he was flipping through the CD bin. I was happy to see him. He was the first prof I had a crush on, though I later figured out he wasn't a full prof, just an adjunct they plugged in to teach lowly Comp cours-es. But it didn't matter, because he was cute. He had long brown hair down to his shoulders, which were quite broad, and he was tall and had nice green eyes that looked always on the verge of filling up with compas-sionate tears for wayward, heartsick freshman girls, of which I was one. Even though it was a Comp course, he would read us poetry in class, and sometimes take us out to the quad so we could sit on benches and write about what we were experiencing at the moment. I wanted to jump his bones, but I was a rookie and shy.

Anyway, here he was two years later, looking about the same except that his hair was shorter and his face a little fuller. I was happy that he re-membered my name. We bullshitted for a while in the store and then he said why don't we get something to eat. He drove us to a Mexican restau-rant where I gorged on a burrito while he caught me up on what he'd been doing for two years. Writing a novel, mostly, he said, and teaching poetry workshops here and there. I didn't know you were a poet, I said. He shrugged and said that he'd had a few poems printed in little maga-zines no one's ever heard of, but that it didn't matter because teaching poetry—and even writing it—was just a business like anything else. That was news to me. I could still remember how passionate he'd been when he read us poems in class. Some of them he knew by heart, like a nice one by Emily Dickinson about God preparing a mansion in heaven for a mouse. He hadn't seemed like a businessman then.

Well, we got onto the subject of Buddhism, probably because I'm always bending people's ears about it these days, and he said that he had an enormous collection of books on the subject and maybe I'd like to poke through them. Cool, I said. Then he suggested we go to his place right now so I could borrow a couple. It was a pretty transparent "come up and see my etchings" ploy, but I didn't care. No harm in checking out his digs, and maybe I'd put celibacy off for a while.

He had a typical struggling writer's small apartment downtown over a Goodwill shop, but I noticed a Bose stereo in the living room so he couldn't have been struggling too much. The bookshelves were wall-to-wall, and he showed me where the religion and philosophy section was. There were plenty of books on Buddhism all right, and I grabbed one that had Karma in the title and started paging through it. Meanwhile Andy had excused himself for a moment. I heard him puttering around in the bedroom. Should I go in there? I wondered. My eyes were looking at the pages of the book, but I was thinking about sex. What would it be like to do him? He didn't seem as cute as two years ago, and I didn't feel much more than a nostalgic attraction. Then I remembered that he was a published poet, and that tipped the scales in his favor.

I heard him coming out of the bedroom and turned to give him a nice fetching smile, and I saw that he was completely naked.

I have to admit it scared me. Was he a nut job? Was he going to try to rape me? But something in his expression put me at ease. He was smiling pleasantly, and his body language wasn't tense or weird. It was like he'd walked into the room wearing a turtleneck and jeans instead of nothing at all. My eyes first went to his dingle—how could they not?—but then I made sure not to stare at it. Find anything you like, he asked?

Okay, I thought, this is not normal, and I am not going to pretend that it is. So what's with the birthday suit, I asked. Oh, jeez, he said, I'm sorry.

Does it bother you? I guess I got naked without even thinking about it. I'm a nudist, and it's such a natural thing to me that sometimes I forget to warn people.

Oh, please. This was so wrong that if I'd had a dick it would have shriveled like a leaky balloon. I gave him my best "whatever" look and said nah, it's no big thing.

Lust was over. The whorls of hair on his chest and belly couldn't hide the fact that he'd gone to flab. He looked better with his clothes on.

He glanced at the book I was holding. You want to borrow that one, he asked? I shoved it back on the shelf. Noo, I said, maybe some other time. Anyway, I just remembered this shit I have to do, so I better get going.

And get going I did. I hopped a bus home and grabbed an overnight bag and told my mom I'd be staying at Claire's, which I often do. It was raining pretty hard by the time I got there and Claire and I watched a couple of old black and white flicks on Turner Classics and ate popcorn while the rain drummed against the windows. She shrieked with laughter when I told her about Andy the pervert. The night had turned chilly so we slept together in Claire's double bed, which girls can do without raising any eyebrows, thank god. We even spooned for warmth, and fell asleep while quietly telling each other stories from our girlhoods. It was a sweet ending to a fucked-up day.

But in the middle of the night there was a pounding on the door, and Claire got up to let in her boyfriend Chris, who was drunk and loud. They had a brief fight but then it got quiet, and I knew Claire would be spending the night on the futon in the living room with Chris. I didn't want to hear them fucking, so I dug my iPod out of my bag and listened to Moby until I drifted off.

*

I woke up to the sound of soft, steady breathing. Claire had returned sometime in the night, probably to escape Chris's beery snores. I felt rested, and lay for a while looking out the window. Claire's bed was just a mattress and box spring on the floor, so all I could see was the top of the neighbor's house and a rectangle of blue sky, but it was enough. Summer's end had brought hurricanes to the south, and here in Pennsyltucky we'd been getting spin-off downpours for a couple of weeks. The ponds and rivers were swollen and the ground was soggy wherever you walked. I wanted the blue sky to last.

When I climbed out of bed Claire groaned a little but otherwise made no sign of waking up. I got dressed and padded out to the living room to find my K-Swisses. They were underneath Chris's smelly T-shirt on the floor next to the futon. I sat in a chair opposite and slipped on my shoes while looking at Claire's loser boyfriend, with his scraggly mustache and long greasy hair, his tattoos and ratty boxers. He'd kicked the comforter off during his restless sleep. It was chilly in the apartment and I considered draping it back over him, but something in the picture irritated me, so I thought fuck it and got up to leave. There would be food in the kitchen, but so what. A bakery not more than two miles away had good sticky buns, and that's what I was after.

I left without waking anyone up, without making a sound, like a ghost vanishing at sunrise. That's how my dad left us. Home at night, gone in the morning. Not even a note. Poof. He was in California now, selling real estate, living with a woman not much older than me, the prick. But I didn't care anymore. Of all the things I might have trouble detaching myself from, my cruddy father was way down on the list.

To get to the bakery you had to walk a few blocks through Claire's neighborhood and then over a bridge spanning a small river—they called it a creek around here—that ran into the mighty Susquehanna. The sun had only been up an hour or so, and the streets were deserted. There was a light breeze, cool to my skin, and puddles shining on the pavement. I guess I felt happy.

When I got to the bridge there were all these people gathered at the railing. Was it a regatta? Had somebody drowned? Then I heard the roar, and as I walked closer I saw that the creek's brown rushing water was dangerously high.

I stepped onto the bridge and grabbed a part of the railing for myself, away from the rabble. There was a carnival atmosphere, people shouting to one another, talking on their cell phones, pointing down at the churning water. I'm not really a misanthrope, but at times like this I wish there weren't so many people in the world. It bothered me that their noise interfered with my listening to the gurgle and rush of the creek. I breathed in deeply, savoring the damp earth smell rising from the muddy water. A fat kid ran behind me yelling something I couldn't make out, calling to a friend or parent. I looked down along the railing and sure enough, half of the people on the bridge were fatties. Slice the blubber off them, just from under their chins, and you could feed an Eskimo family for a month.

A trio of high school boys was a few feet away, whooping it up and making jokes. I'm pretty sure they noticed me and wanted to look cool, but I paid no attention. The river moved swiftly beneath us, carrying tree limbs, plastic fencing, a tire, a baseball cap. I saw lumber, maybe from a chicken coop or shed that had been washed out of somebody's back yard.

I felt the sun on my hair, the wind in my face. There was no hurricane here, and the floodwaters had not reached my feet. I was ready to turn and head to the other side of the bridge, ready for sticky buns and maybe a cupcake.

But before I let go of the railing I noticed something else coming down the river. It was a chest of drawers, painted bright pink and yellow. It was tall rather than wide, and not too big. With those colors, probably a little girl's dresser. Hey, Matt, yelled one of the high schoolers, what's your dresser doing in the creek? There was laughter, but it trailed off. The dresser was floating on its back, and you could see that the drawers were plastered with stickers. I bent over the railing, looking hard, and saw images I remembered from my own childhood—the Little Mermaid, Care Bears, Cookie Monster. I watched—we all watched—as this casualty of the flood, this lost dresser from a little girl's bedroom, disappeared under the bridge.

It was quiet now. No more jokes, the carnival atmosphere gone. I left my perch and headed for the bakery.

There was a line, but I took a number and waited. Outside, my goodies in hand, I waited again, for a bus. It took me home, and for some reason

I was breathing hard as I put my key in the door lock. Mom, I called, but there was no answer. I put my bag of pastries on the kitchen table and went upstairs to my bedroom. I threw myself on the bed and reached over the side to pull a cardboard box out from underneath. From the box I extracted Oliver, the long-eared, white-plush rabbit I had slept with all my life until just a few years ago. Oliver was tattered and dusty, but I held him tightly to my chest.

When the tears came I wasn't surprised. But it was fine. I'd get over it. ●

Truth-Sayer

2606

by Heather Parry

SHE WAS IN UP TO THE SECOND SET OF KNUCKLES BEFORE HER GAG REFLEX finally began to relent. Despite all the protestations of her body, desperate to not let her enter into that world again, the cud of hastily crumpled paper started to slide down her throat, its edges nicking her soft tissue as it went. Maps of tears ran from her eyelids to her chin but there was no one else in the bathroom to see; only her own reflection, already panda-eyed and crimson with effort. She tried to swallow, rubbing her throat as if she was a cat, all the while saying to herself *eat it, you idiot, you need it*.

It was halfway down when it stopped and she panicked. The face in the mirror took on a mauve tint, the eyes widening so that she could see the broken capillaries. Not willing to end her days in such a pathetic situation (*just think of the headlines: freak suffocates self in mad bathroom antics*) she threw herself against the side of the bath, breaking a rib on the stained side of the tub. The damp clump of paper stuck itself to the tiles in front of her and she could breathe once again.

She grabbed that first lungful of air, heaving and choking on it, and watched the words *whole milk* smear against the grouting. The pain spread all over her torso, and she wept quietly for a little while. Was it so difficult to start smoking once you had given up – was that first drag of nicotine an ordeal, or a relief? The first drink after half a decade away; did it burn your throat like the first shot of vodka?

This was like beginning all over again.

Her stomach fell from her torso to her toes; as the warmth spread over her she knew what was coming.

"Miss, there's wet all over that girl. There's wet all over her."

"Are you okay, my dear?"

"Miss it's dripping on the floor."

Her head buzzed and fizzed as she slowly blinked. *Say you spilled your drink. Say it's sweat. Say anything say anything say anything.*

It was coming out.

"I've wet myself, Miss."

She tried not to go out at playtime but with a fresh pair of jeans on and pants from Lost Property, Miss Webster, smiling, shoved her out there alone.

BABY PEE PANTS STUPID BABY IDIOT.

She let go of the tenseness of her body and became a marionette, dancing a ballet between their hands; it was a piece that she knew well, a practiced symphony of which they were masters. It began and she moved slowly, her mother's music in her mind, her body turning with every shove, her toes en pointe as her head snapped to the side, her fingers stretched upwards with grace as she felt forward on grazed knees and felt a kick at her chest.

At lunch she ran from the classroom with her book bag and locked the stall behind her. With her back against the cold ceramic lip she tried to read to pass the time. Why couldn't she have said something else, or nothing at all? Why were her own words so inextricably nailed to the truth?

Spread out on the page in front of her, the letters looked so harmless. The peaks of a T and the troughs of a P created landscapes in every line. They were beautiful, intoxicating, satisfying words. They were the opposite of her words, childish and naïve. She tore the page down the middle and crammed the liberated half in her mouth just as the room exploded with excited footsteps and her puppeteers gathered all around her stall. She scrabbled upwards onto the toilet and lifted her feet, hiding herself as they threw her name around, bruising it. The book bag was slowly lifted upwards so it would not rustle and give her away. She chewed on the wet paper to keep herself from howling.

It tasted rough and fetid, that very first handful of literature, and it made her retch and weep as she salivated onto it and bit down with her teeth. Both paper and fiction were alien to her young mouth and the cud kept trying to escape, expelling itself past her lips and dropping between her thighs. She kept the sobs silent lest they hear her crying; the breathless chokes lingered in the back of her mouth like the taste of metal when you run. She tried again, silently ripping out more pages and pushing them in, each scrunched up like a scoop of ice cream, the off-white of the paper doing little to trick her into believing that they were strawberry and mint chocolate chip. Beyond the toilet door, finally, the bell sounded the end of lunchtime and the footsteps of her tormenters scattered. She swallowed but the mass wouldn't go; it took another minute to get the pulp all the way down then it sat like bread inside her; a satisfying, comforting clump. After the first handful it got easier, and with five pages of fiction unfurling in her stomach she felt sure that nothing else would come up.

As the fantasy and falsehoods melted in her stomach she found herself able to use them. They were the white lies and outright fibs that she needed. She passed the rest of the day without bruises, bites or hair pulls, without spilling her unbridled honesty. The words of others weighed down her own. And so it began.

It quickly became a compulsion, like sucking her thumb. She worked through the picture books of her infancy, tearing the drawings up into tiny pieces and letting them dissolve under her tongue, then moved up to longer stories, chewing each one like a piece of overcooked meat. For an entire year her mother stood perplexed by the ever-widening gaps on her bookshelves, until the afternoon following a particularly vicious day of teasing at school, when her ink-stained daughter vomited half a Jilly Cooper on her living room carpet.

As she studied for her GCSEs, she took a peculiar joy in the watery mush in her mouth. She had become a connoisseur; she could tell a *roman a clef* from a gothic horror just with a few licks of a line or two, and as characters ate their meals her taste buds would dance to the descriptions of the dishes. Yet, like all vices, it was no good for her, and over the years her weary digestive tract began to strain with the effort of even a pamphlet; long gone were the days of consuming a novella in just a week. Her insides ached constantly and she took hours to excavate the literature from her body; *it's all poison and poems in there* said her doctor when she was just 17, warning her that she would die before 25 if she didn't give it up.

And so she had, more or less, because dealing with her issue had become easier with age—or rather, the puzzle pieces of the world had shifted around her and she understood why people hated it so. As a child she couldn't comprehend how much humans wrapped themselves in lies and took comfort in myths of their own making. Her words, so impossible to keep inside, were sharp and pricked the balloons of ego, deflating the listener; of course they were angry. She would have been angry too.

In her adulthood, she still said all the things that people didn't want to hear—there was no way to stop it, beyond the slow suicide of the pages—but grown ups, it turned out, were better than children at ignoring the things that pierced their self-delusions. She had learned to turn away from situations where the truth was not welcome; she refused to go shopping with friends, and got involved in no disputes amongst family, and though many of her friends were in the arts she would see no plays, hear no music and taste no food that they had created. She rid her room, then her house, of the books that posed such a temptation, like an addict freeing her life of paraphernalia. She didn't so much avoid the problem as maneuver carefully around it.

Of course, there were lapses. The stab of the question "You like him, don't you?" coming down the phone line from her newly betrothed friend was only narrowly avoided by consuming the very wedding invitation that she had called to decline. When her freshly bald and chemotherapy-exhausted mother asked her how she looked, she ran to the bathroom, took the emergency short story collection (Murakami; more palatable than most) from her handbag and had shoved two entire tales into her mouth before she could emerge with no answer, just a smile and a nod. Men went flying out of her bed as if just given wings; most of them she wouldn't miss.

With him, it had been different.

She sat at a café one slow Saturday morning, drawing flowers in the condensation, as there were none outside.

"Are you reading this?" he asked, his fingers already reaching for the paper on her table.

"I was hoping to," she replied, not turning towards him, "but now I feel like I have to let you take it, and if I do I'll have nothing to look at while I drink my coffee, so I'll probably rush it and not enjoy it anyway. So really, I don't want you to have it, but I'm not reading it right now, so I suppose I have to say no, I'm not reading this."

She paused to allow for the shock of the rudeness, that brief moment where no one says anything, but before she could glance toward him he slid his body in next to hers.

"How about we read it together, then?"

He goaded her into spilling her opinions with the turn of every page, and she felt playful for the first time in years. He grinned as she spoke her uncaged truths and laughed at what she said. As he got up to leave, the paper long discarded on the floor, something in her panicked; she wanted to keep feeling that way, like a particle caught in the sunlight.

She blurted it out. He smiled. They saw each other every day that week.

He caught her words with cupped hands and drank them down, enjoying her more with every one. He served her steak; she said it was like chewing a shoe. They threw both pieces at the wall and watched it slide down over takeaway pizza. He gave up smoking when she told him that it made him look arrogant.

She had intended to keep her singular condition to herself, to keep her life with him free of all that horror, but at Christmas he told her he was going to work drinks at a local bar and when she called in, tipsy and turned on after a nearby night out with friends, he was not there. He found her collapsed in a puddle of sheer agony underneath her sparsely decorated tree, heaving and baying, and handed over the last-minute gift that he'd left the event to buy her. She spilled everything out during a sleepless night of truths and history, and showed him the scars that the lies of others had caused her; it tormented her that others could so easily weave tales when she could not, and he promised he would never thrust the sharpened blade of fabrication into her soft skin, even for good reason.

At New Year she packed her things in boxes and made his home into hers. Slowly, the shelves of her library became full once more, and in four years she ate not a single word.

Fuck, she thought, as her fingers probed the tender area where the black bruise already blossomed, bringing to mind the shrill shrieks of child-hood assault. She was pissed off that it was a tasteless shopping list that broke her fast, even if it had ended up sliding down the wall and resting on the moldy side of the bath. She could have probably grabbed a newspaper, the cute note left on the kitchen table, even, as she heard his keys jiggle in the lock—he always struggled to get them working, even though hers unlocked it first time—but she had panicked looking around at everything she stood to lose, and had bolted for the bathroom and locked the door behind her. His keys hit the hall table and he called out to her, and she felt that familiar sense of expulsion begin; she needed words to keep it down.

The list.

She had been cooking three-bean chili for them both when the first kernel of uncertainty popped, the list crammed in her pocket from a trip to the grocery store to pick up tortillas and sour cream. He said he was going to drop off a library book; she mindlessly glanced toward the door as it slammed itself shut. The cold emptiness descended. The prickly heat of deception spread across her face and down her neck. He'd left the novel on the top of his bag. She had waited ten heartbeats for him to come back, to grab it and go, but he did not. The grief of undeniable betrayal burst out of her and splattered into the sink.

It was a small lie, a nothing. To others, meaningless. But as she stared at the book, parts of her life began to peel away. She had to know. She had to.

She left the door open behind her as she ran down the stairs.

She barely went beyond the end of the street and there he was. It would have been better if there had been a woman—a man, even. A meeting. A drug deal. Anything. But there was not; there was only him, sitting on the park bench alone with a cigarette in his mouth, doing nothing, just reveling with dark spite in doing, for a moment, what she could not: in lying. He stubbed the burning fragment out under his sole and she began to run home. He wouldn't be far behind.

She reached out and plucked the paper mush from the wall, resigning herself to the fact. Beyond the door, he heeled off his shoes and let them kick against the skirting board as he called her name again. The inky mess in her hand seemed to wriggle with anticipation; a rotten piece of fruit covered in maggots. In it, she could see the months ahead of her; the receipts collected in her wallet for emergencies, the notes she would leave in torn library books, explaining that she needed the pages more than the next reader. She felt that bloating feeling in her stomach; as it grew, the Human Resources Director at work would email over a clarification of her maternity allowance, over which she would silently weep.

Yet still, as she looked around at the bathroom that they had decorated badly over a stressful weekend in May, she couldn't bear to face the other option. Perhaps she would eventually forget what she'd seen, and let the paranoia of knowing slide away from her like ice. Perhaps she would give it up all over again, her stomach recovering and leaving her happy. Perhaps she would one day accept the fact that this thing, this skill that she didn't have, was something that he did for fun, not to hurt her, but because he could.

She forced the crumpled page into her mouth and swallowed. ●

The Flexible Persona

1970

by Henry Marchand

THEY COME INTO TOWN FROM THE WOODS ON SUMMER NIGHTS. MOM SAYS they're hippies, and Dad calls them communists. I think they're interesting. Especially the girls. They're not like girls in town, and it isn't just because they wear shorts made of blue jeans or dresses that hang loose on them and that you can kind of see through when the sun's not completely down yet, and you know that some of them don't wear underwear. I mean it is that they look different, yeah, but they also move different, somehow, and you can tell they think it's kind of funny how people look at them. And they don't look away. They smile at you. They smile at me, and it feels like they might be laughing at me but it feels good, too. None of the girls in town smile at me, except mom and that's not the same because she's not a girl, she's a mom and a woman.

Mom likes them, I can tell. Dad sure doesn't. He says they need to grow up, wash up, and get their asses home or down to the recruitment office. Mom tells him not everyone thinks like he does, but he says Americans do. I asked Mom if the hippies aren't Americans and she said of course they are. She says they're young and see things in a new way. She says it with a kind of a soft look in her eyes and her voice gets quieter. That's when I know she likes them.

Dad's never quiet when he talks about them. I think the hippies don't like war, but I don't think Dad likes war so it's pretty confusing. He was in a war and he always says it was a terrible thing. I don't know why he would want the hippies to be in a war, except maybe because they don't wash enough and maybe Dad hates dirty people more than I knew he did. He does get mad when I don't clean behind my ears and tells me potatoes will grow back there.

Because it's summer now and school's out, I go to the Acme market with Mom when she buys groceries. Usually we go in the morning, but this morning she had ladies from the VFW at the house to talk about sending food baskets to the families of soldiers who are missing in the war. I guess there are three families in town that just got calls from the government. The soldiers aren't dead, Mom told me. It's just that in the jungle some- times soldiers get separated from each other and someone gets lost. I know this is like when we go to the city for my new eyeglasses and I can never let go of her hand; I could be taken away by a bad person, before a good person could find me and take me to the police station. In the jun- gle I know there aren't many people at all. Just animals like tigers and go- rillas. And maybe if there are people they're all soldiers and when you're lost enemy soldiers might find you before the good soldiers do. I wonder why that wouldn't mean the missing soldiers might be dead. Don't enemies kill each other in a war?

I don't think the hippies would kill anyone. They wear those peace signs on chains around their necks and have peace sign patches on the back pockets of their shorts. I saw a girl once with just a bathing suit top on above her shorts and on her belly she had a peace sign drawn in magic marker. It made me wonder if it tickled when she drew it on, and how she could do it since she would have to be looking at it upside-down. Maybe someone else drew it there. I don't think anyone who draws peace signs on people or who lets other people draw on them on would kill someone. Dad might be wrong thinking it would be good for hippies to go to the war.

After the VFW ladies left, my mom remembered there were things she needed from the store. I said I would go, but she said I'm too young. In a couple of years, she said. It's only a little way to the market but there are two big streets and only one of them has a traffic light between our house and there. I know I could cross them both fine. Mom is just nervous. She doesn't like that other moms' sons are getting lost in the jungle.

We didn't go to the market right away. Grandma called from Florida and she always talks a long time. I had to talk to her too, and she wanted to know if I got grades in school this year and what I was doing this summer. Then grandpa got on and asked if I had any girlfriends. He said a man has to start young if he wants to find one that will last. Grandma laughed and I didn't know what to say. My friends are the ones I've always had and only Janey Hirsch is a girl. That's not what grandpa means, though. He's just joking, but it makes me feel weird. When she gets back on the phone mom hugs me a second and tells grandpa to lighten up, he's making me uncomfortable. Then she says, well, put mom back on I have to get going.

The streetlights were coming on when we left for the Acme market. I like that time when the day's not over but you feel the air getting cooler and the big moths come out to fly around the lights, and then the bats come to swoop around, trying to catch the moths. I haven't ever seen a bat catch a moth. That would be cool.

When we got to the market there were three hippies sitting on the curb near the new doors that open by themselves, two girls and a boy. The girls had long straight hair and the boy did, too, but his was black and the girls' hair was like Mom's, a kind of gold with red mixed in. They looked at us and smiled. They were smoking cigarettes and one of the girls had a deposit bottle of Pepsi-Cola in her hand. I guess that was what they came to the market to buy, cigarettes and soda. Maybe they got the money to buy things by saving soda bottles and getting the deposits back. Dad says none of them work, that's for sure. My friend Andy bought a model of Napoleon Solo with money he got by returning bottles; you can find empty ones all over if you look for them.

The boy hippie whistled at my mom. I looked at her and she looked surprised and her face got red as we went into the market through the open doors. The boy hippie laughed and one of the girls said he was so uncool. The store was cold inside because of the air conditioner. It made me feel dizzy. Mom took the list she'd written from her purse and told me to get a shopping cart.

When we were done we had two bags and I carried one. The hippies weren't outside the store anymore but I saw them standing in the parking lot near the Mr. Donut shop, smoking and talking with some kids I knew went to the high school. One of them was my friend Andy's brother Bill.

Dinner was going to be spaghetti and meatballs and garlic bread. I was going to drink a Pepsi-Cola that I got for helping with the groceries. Dad came home from work and washed up, then came into the kitchen and got a can of beer from the refrigerator. He always drinks Rheingold beer. He sat at the table and mom made the meatballs at the counter by the sink and he asked how the day was for us on the home front. Mom said fine and I told him about going to the store and the air conditioner that made me dizzy and the hippie who whistled at mom. Dad took the beer can away from his lips and a little beer spilled out and ran down his chin. He wiped it with his hand and said, Where? It was nothing, mom told him. Like hell, he said, and he put his hand on my shoulder. Where was this, he said, and his fingers hurt my shoulder a little. Outside the market, I said. My mom wiped her hands on her apron and her face was very serious. She said, Ben. He looked at her, but his hand still held my shoulder. I didn't say anything about it hurting. My dad stood and let go of me. He reached down and picked up the beer can and drank until the can was empty. Then he set it on the counter by the sink and looked at me and said, Show me.

He parked the car by the market but it was by the end with the store where he bought beer, and I told him they were over by the Mr. Donut when we were leaving. He told me to come with him and we got out of the car and walked over there. Look around, he said. Do you see him? I looked, but there were only cars parked outside the donut shop and inside I could see only a couple of people at the counter and the old German lady who was always working there. I mean it was like she never left, like she lived there and worked there too. They aren't here, I said. Come on, he said and he started walking around the building. On the other side near the big garbage can the boy hippie and Andy's brother Bill were standing with cans of beer in their hands. That's him with Bill, I said, the girls must have gone back to the woods. I don't care about them, my dad said. His voice scared me. He didn't yell but I knew he was really mad.

What's the problem, Andy's brother Bill said. He knew me and my dad, but he must have wondered why we were there. I didn't really know, either. You're Bill Douglas's kid, my father said. Bill nodded. Leave, my father told him. Bill looked at the boy hippie and back at my dad, then at me and he ran. You, my dad said.

The boy hippie drank from his beer can. He and my dad were facing each other and I saw that he wasn't really a boy, he was older. Older than Andy's brother, and definitely older than the hippie girls. I know you? he said. My dad moved so fast I didn't know he did, but the beer can bounced on the ground and foamed on the gravel by the garbage can. Who the fuck are you to whistle at my wife, my dad said. Dad! I said. He never used that word, and his voice sounded like he'd turned into someone else. I started shaking and I looked around for help but there was no one. There was just the three of us, and I wanted to be back home with Mom.

I whistle at whoever I want to, the other man said. He was wearing a vest made of something black and shiny with no shirt underneath. There was a silver peace sign hanging on a chain around his neck. It hung down on the middle of his chest where he had a lot of sweaty black hair. He was wearing blue jeans and black boots. My dad was wearing blue jeans too and a white t-shirt and sneakers, like he always did after he got home from work. The other man was a little taller. Dad, I said.

You don't whistle at my wife, my dad said. It was like he didn't know I was there anymore.

The other man held up his hands and grinned. Hey, I'm sorry, he said. Forget it. Don't be an asshole.

My dad grabbed the chain around the man's neck. The man stepped back and fell and the chain broke. He got back to his feet really fast and they looked at each other. My dad held the peace sign in his hand.

I fought for this country, you piece of shit, he said. I went to war and I saw men die. I killed men and watched other men kill. You have no right—

I was crying. The other man looked at me and at my dad and pushed back his long black hair with one of his hands. He pointed at my dad.

Me too, he said. I was there. I was there and I just got back and you're here with your wife and your kid and you call me a piece of shit. What do you know, man? Your war was different. I come back and my wife doesn't want me. I'm *glad* I got no kids, because I wouldn't know what to tell them they should believe in. You tell this guy here war is good and noble? I can't do that. There's no Adolf Hitler out there, the Japs ain't dropping bombs.

The man dropped his hands to his sides. I didn't mean to insult your wife, he said. I didn't mean to make you mad. He smiled. I whistle at 'em all, man. It's nothing personal. He looked at me again, and then at my dad.

She's pretty, I bet, he said. Your boy's a good-lookin' kid, and he don't get it from you. My dad laughed. I didn't know what was happening.

My dad gave the man his peace sign back. He held onto it a second before he let it go, and they looked at each other. It felt like there was a secret they knew, and it made them sad. But just a second ago they seemed happy together.

Sorry about the beer, my dad said.

I'll find another one, the man said.

My dad put his hand on my shoulder and said Come on, and we walked back to the car.

When we got home dinner was on the table and mom looked at us and dad said, It's all right. She nodded and wiped her eyes and we sat down to eat. •

Light on Dimmed Bodies

by K. L. Morris

AT NIGHT, I CREEP OUT OF BED TO LOOK AT HIM. MY HUSBAND IS WHERE I left him—in the kitchen chair against the living room wall. His hands rest in his lap, palms down on his thighs. His face is empty.

I crouch in front of him, send one tentative finger to test his cheek. Is it warm or cold? But his chest rises and falls, and my finger halts. It doesn't matter if he is warm or cold. It doesn't matter if he's breathing. My husband is a body now. The rest of him has gone.

I leave him there and go back to bed.

In the morning, Selma comes to check him out. When she opens the door, the sun streams into the house like an interruption, like a shout in a library. It shines on Dick where he's immobilized on his chair, and my heart jumps. When she closes it, everything stills again. Our tiny house has always been dim. I never wash the windows, and I keep the curtains drawn. Now, I don't want people coming by and seeing him. Before, I didn't want people coming by and seeing me. Where he sits in the corner, it is dark and quiet. Like him.

Selma stands before him for a few minutes, her palms denting her wide, flabby hips. She cocks her head. On his chair, Dick doesn't respond. Normally, he would make a crack about her tiny hands and her large ass, but his body only hangs there.

"You're right," says Selma. "This ain't him. But it sure is weird to look at." Her hand snaps out and slaps him across the face. He rocks back and forth on the chair, but otherwise doesn't move. She isn't strong enough to knock him over. "I always wanted to do that," she says.

"Don't do that again, okay? I'm still here."

Selma shrugs big, her heavy shoulders heaving her breasts up and down. "Sure thing. But it ain't like I slapped you," she says.

"Where'd he go, you think?"

"His mind, maybe," says Selma. "Or maybe he just poofed away. I never really thought there was much there to begin with to be honest." She reaches out to prod his face again, but catches sight of me and stops herself. "You checked his pulse and his breathing and all that?"

I nod. He's still warm, heart still beating. It's just—he's a body now, and not a man. "What'm I supposed to do now? Now he's gone?"

Selma shrugs again. Every time she does this, I get the willies. She's got so *much* to her body. It makes me uncomfortable watching it all go. "Find another?"

"Selma, I ain't like you. I can't just go around replacing one with the next with the next. I liked this one. He was supposed to stick around."

"Technically, he hasn't gone anywhere. Maybe you can list him with a medical condition or something? Get some money for him. Buy a new front door. Your lock sticks."

"Who's going to put the door in?" I ask.

"I'll send my guy over. He can help."

"I'd rather have Dick."

Selma sweeps her arm out, like she's throwing candies at a parade, and I watch the fat on her arms jiggle. God, I never want to be that fat. "He's right here, babycakes."

When the sun goes down, I lie in bed, but I can't sleep. Dick is still in the living room. He's not going to come to bed. He used to do that, when he was still...animated. He used to lay out in the easy chair and wait to go to bed for a while. He knew I'd stay up with him, waiting in my little kitchen chair in the living room. He didn't have one show he watched—he liked marathons. A marathon of anything—*Ice Road Truckers* or *Happy Days*. He didn't care. So long as there was a bunch of episodes, back to back to back.

I never liked that. I liked my television in tiny sips—one episode at a time, and I always watched it from my chair. Even when we got that new Internet thing—the one where you can watch whole television seasons in one sitting, if you want—I'd still watch just one. Dick hated that. He wanted me to watch more with him, but I was sure all the sitting would make my behind flabby.

I want to go and get Dick, bring him in the room with me, but if he falls halfway here, I won't be able to pick him up.

I cannot sleep, not with him out there, and if you don't sleep, you're eyes get puffy and blue. I've seen it on TV. I didn't sleep last night, either. I grab the edges of the blanket and pull them around myself, then I go out of the bedroom again. He's facing the couch. I lay down there, so he can see me, and then I can sleep.

Selma is back in the morning. She taps me on the shoulder to wake me up. The sun is sitting on the living room windowsill, but the curtains keep it there, block it from coming in any farther. The day outside is a secret I don't want to hear.

"Babycakes, I done some googling, and I have stuff to show you." She prods my side with her hip, and when I'm slow to get out of the way, she says, "Shove over, so I can sit down." I spent the whole night on the couch, with plenty of room, but with Selma here, the entire living room fills up.

She lays the papers she brought on the coffee table. She has to move the beer bottles Dick left there, and a pair of reading glasses, and some crumpled up receipts from my purse. When she shoves them out of the way, some stuff falls off the other side, but I don't catch it.

"Look, I was trying to find out what could have happened with your boy over there." Selma looks to the corner, just to make sure Dick is still there. He is. "And I found a couple things it could be."

She sticks her finger on one page. "This one is a thing you can probably get money for. If he's cata—catatonic? That how you say that?"

"I don't know," I tell her. "It's a funny looking word."

"That one you can get money for. But that just means he's been shocked stupid. Kind of boring, really, and unless he saw you with your push-up off, I don't know what could give him a scare bad enough to do that." She nods towards Dick, like he's a secret we're keeping.

"But there's this one, too." She pushes the catatonic papers to the side, right into an old beer spill, and pulls a stack of new ones to the front. She turns to me with a big grin, but when Selma smiles, it always looks like her teeth are caught in the trenches in a war, like they're being eaten by her cheeks. "This one's astral projection," she says. "This one happens if the spirit leaves the body, you know?"

"The spirit?"

"You know. Like the—like the soul or whatever."

"How does it leave?" My hand is sneaking up my sternum. I thought you were connected to your body, I didn't know your soul could escape.

Selma shrugs. "It doesn't just *go*. You send it out from your physical form, just for a while. But I think something went wrong with him."

"But Dick doesn't even know how to do that!"

Selma looks at me, then at him. Clearly, she says with her eyes, Dick can do things we didn't know about.

"I like the other one," I say. "The cat one."

"This one makes more sense, honey."

"What would Dick's spirit want to do out of his body?"

"I don't know," says Selma. "Go for a walk?"

"If it just went for a walk, why didn't it come back?" It's been two days.

"Maybe it can't?" she says. "Maybe it got trapped or something."

We read the papers, and they say if that happens, you need to make the body 'open' so the soul can climb back inside. For the rest of the day, we try and open him up to the return of his spirit. We start with his mouth. It's been closed so long; it's hard to pry open. I have to push my fingers between his teeth, and then Selma sticks a rag between them to hold his mouth that way. We open his eyes. We use tape on his eyelashes to keep them that way. I worry that they'll dry out, but Selma thinks he'll be fine. We even turn his hands over, so they're palm up, like he's waiting for something. Then Selma lights a candle.

"Why?" I ask.

"You always light a candle," she says.

She sticks it on the tiny table next to Dick, pushing some water glasses and a few plates out of the way. When Dick watched television, this was where I ate dinner. Now that he's gone, I don't eat anymore.

"What if his spirit's scared of the light? They always say don't go to the light."

"Different light," says Selma, but she moves the candle anyway. She doesn't blow it out.

An hour passes. Selma is restless. She is not good at sitting still like me. She picks at her fingernails, and brushes her fingers through her hair, creases and uncreases her pants. This last movement is amazing. She grabs a tiny pinch of the denim and squeezes it, then watches as it goes back to normal. She must be squeezing her skin, too, because Selma's pants are so tight, there's no extra space anywhere in them, not even for air. If I was her spirit, I'd feel suffocated.

Finally, she stands up. "You'll let me know if the candle goes out?" she says.

I tell her sure, but I don't understand the significance of that. Then she leaves. In his corner, Dick doesn't move. His eyes are open, but I close mine to make a picture in my mind. I picture the way he looked when he used to come home from work, before he lost his job and things got sour for a while. I picture when he scooped me up in his arms and twirled me around and said, "Jeez, you're light like a bird!" In my head, I am always wearing a white dress, and in my head, he always brings the sun inside with him. But with my eyes open, I can see that my clothes aren't white, they're gray. Seeing the way my thighs squish out around me, I know that I'm not light like a bird, and I never was. And the light never comes inside because I never invite it.

I sleep on the couch again, but I barely sleep. I'm hungry, and I can feel Dick watching me, with his eyes taped like that. It makes me uncomfortable now. What was he doing when he slinked off outside of his body? Where was his soul going?

I get up and go to him. He is the same as we left him. The candle is out, I didn't blow it out before going to sleep, and the wick is gently smoking. I can never remember if that means it just went out, or it's ready to be lit again.

I pick at the edges of the scotch tape with a fingernail, until it starts to come lose. It peels off in strips, like when someone drops it back on the roll without folding an edge. One of his eyelashes pulls free of his eyelid. I stare at it, sitting on the pad of my thumb, safe against me, protected from the rest of the world with a piece of tape. I press it close with my tongue and keep it there.

When the tape is off his eyes, I take Dick's hands and put them on my hips. When Dick was—Dick used to start at my hips and then climb my ribs like ladders, until his fingers got to the edges of my bra, where my body starts to flare out again. Then he'd pretend his fingers lost their grip and they'd start to fall, down onto my hips, where they'd bounce like they were on a trampoline. I liked the part where he climbed my ribs, but I hated when he made his fingers bounce on my hips, like I was fat like Selma.

Tonight, I hold his hands still and whisper into his lips, "Come back, baby, come back."

In the morning, his eyelash is still trapped against my thumb. I push it against my knuckle to keep it there.

Selma has not called since she left last night, and it is late morning when I wake up. I suspect she will not come today. I get a chair from the kitchen and set it down in front of Dick. When I sit in it, we are close to each other, but not close enough that our knees touch. In the morning, it is harder to pretend it's him. The tiny bits of light that escape the dark curtains make it clear he's somewhere else.

I push his eyelids back. His eyes are still blank, but it doesn't matter. I want to know what he is thinking. I want to know where he went. "Dick, where did you go?" I think his eyes look the same as when he lost his job, when he used to look from the TV to me. When he was bored and his breath was sour. When he wanted me to do things and got mad at me when I didn't.

The door rattles, and I was wrong. Selma is shoving her way in. She hates that door because the lock sticks and we lost all our keys. Turning the doorknob is like a code.

"Did he do anything?" she says, before she even gets inside. She uses her fat behind to close the door, her arms full of paper bags. "I brought you some food."

I don't tell her I won't eat. She goes past me to put the bags in the kitchen. I haven't eaten since Dick...since Dick did what he did, but I think that's good. Maybe this will bring him back. I never liked eating, so Dick made a deal with me. So long as he watched TV and left me alone, I would eat. I hated it when he watched me. I think he tried to make me eat more by watching all that TV, but it didn't matter because I am a slow eater. I can take a whole episode to eat one Ritz cracker. My eating was a secret between us. When Selma comes back in the room, she lays a hand on my shoulder, like she caught me in the middle of something and feels bad. The flesh on her fingers looks tight, and she painted her nails an eggplant purple. I push back from her—back from Dick.

We go to the couch and sit down. For a minute, it is silent, but Selma can never be silent for long. She picks at the blanket on the couch.

"You sleep here again?"

"I don't like sleeping by myself."

Selma eyes Dick in the corner. "He freaks me out. Even if it was my guy, I can tell you, I would not be sleeping in here. Damn thing like a mummy."

"Don't talk about him like that."

Selma puts her hand on my knee. "Honey, he ain't there."

I take my knee back, and don't look at the way Selma makes her face, like I hurt her. "Where do you think he went?"

"Hell if I know," she says. "But I can tell you what he might come back for." She snickers a little, like she's keeping a secret, but I know what she means. "I'll tell you, I've had men leave me before, but they always come back. And they always come back for the same thing." She grabs the fat around her waist and twists herself like a washing machine. "*This,*" she goes.

"That's what we were doing when he left," I say.

Selma looks at me good and long before she bursts into big laughs, laughs that shake her belly up and down. "I can tell you, girl, if that's what you were doing when he left, then you can't have been doing it right!"

I think—*She doesn't know anything.* I think—*Could she be right?*

When Selma goes, I go back to the chair in front of Dick. There is something about him that frightens me. At first, I am scared to touch him. Touching him will be different now, different from when Selma and I tried to make him open, and different from last night, when I was worried about him.

I touch just his forearm first; it is smooth. Room temperature. It doesn't feel the way a person is supposed to feel, but it doesn't feel bad, either. Then I go down to his wrist, holding the bones between my fingers. Dick is big, much bigger than me, and I can't go all the way around him.

I never noticed his hand before. There is a lot of hair on it. It's thin, and it makes me uncomfortable. I let go of his hand and grab his bicep instead, where his shirt covers it.

I scoot forward, in the chair, until our knees brush. Then, very carefully, I climb into his lap. I straddle him; we're chest to chest. I put my hands on his shoulders.

"Dick, honey, come back."

This time, I kiss him. His lips are like his hands. They aren't warm or cold. They're like plastic. Soft plastic.

"Dick, baby." I brush them with my tongue. He doesn't do anything, but he doesn't push me away.

On the night he—on that night, he woke me up because he wanted sex. I woke up when his sloppy hand pinched the lamp on. I never let him have the light on for sex, just like I never let him take all of my clothes off at one time. He said, "Sh, baby, you're beautiful." He had his hand between my legs before I was all the way awake, and when I pushed against him to turn off the light, he put his lips against my ear and whispered and held my wrist. "Sh, baby, you're beautiful. I want to see you."

It happened the same way you spread butter over toast. The butter starts out thick, but it gets real thin. One minute, he was pressed against my side, then he thinned out. His touches became brushes, his words smeared into breathing, his fingers stopped probing and started stuttering, and then he just—stopped. I led him to the kitchen chair, my kitchen chair, where I could get him water or aspirin if he wanted. He sat down, and he didn't stand up. He was done.

But now—I want him back. In his lap, my crotch brushes his. I'm whispering in his mouth and licking his lips. I grab his arms, and wrap them around my waist. My whole lower half knows what it's doing now, it's moving by itself, so I pay attention to his lips. Dick always liked kisses.

His mouth is open, and I am brave. Tonight, I put my tongue inside it. It's dry in there. I feel his tongue, like a piece of putty lying on the bottom of his mouth. Then the roof of his mouth and the sides of his teeth. I tell myself—*Spread your spit all over!* A person can't live with a mouth dry like this. I brush his teeth with my tongue, and then I taste the rag. The rag that Selma and I put there. I had forgotten about it. It's wedged between one side of his teeth, and it's dried out, like his mouth. It tastes sour and old. I think maybe it is the reason his mouth is so dry. I pull it out with my hand, and when I move, his arms fall from my waist, like dead weight.

I am not like him, but I feel like I am. I feel everything pushing down on me so that moving my arms is hard, moving my legs is hard. I used to get like this sometimes, and Dick would give me kisses and bring me water and help. But he's not here now.

"Wake up, baby, wake up," I say. I tap his cheek with my fingers. "Wake up, baby, I need you." I tap harder. He does not wake up for me. My kisses do not wake him up, my movements against his crotch do not wake him up. I wrap my lips around his and kiss harder and deeper, but his teeth are closed now, they are bars against me, keeping me out. Keeping him in. My tongue cannot get past, no matter how hard I press, but maybe my air can, maybe my air can wake him up. I draw a deep, deep breath, and when I exhale, I realize I am screaming.

Selma finds me on the couch, my face sticky with sweat and my cheek numb. She asks me if I have eaten, and I tell her no. She hardly looks at Dick.

When she comes to the couch, she lays a hand on my knee, I tell her get out.

"Therese, baby. Please."

"Get out, Selma, get out."

"Just eat something for me, babycakes. Just try a cracker or something. Then I'll go. I promise."

"Get out, Selma. Get out."

She leaves. The sun sets. I go to Dick.

He is just a body, I think. I stare at the patches of hair on his hands, the ones I could not look at before. I look at the tiny mole beneath his eye, and for the first time I really let myself hate it, the way I always wanted to.

I pick flecks of skin off his chapped lips, and look at the tiny brown spots decorating his scalp line, where his hair is receding. You can see them now, now that his hair is running away. You can see how ugly he is.

The pores across his nostrils are huge, as if they've been stretched out. At his jawbone, his skin hangs heavy, like a rug someone is beating, and the texture is the same as a rug. I won't ever touch it again. I am ashamed of every time I touched every part of him in the past. The spots under his ears, where I was kissing last night, are covered in tiny patches of wiry gray hair. It makes my mouth fill with spit to think that I placed my tongue there.

"Who are you?" I ask him.

He has hairs everywhere. Not just his hands, but on his belly, too. I have felt it before. And in his armpits, and even around his...even around *that*. I am between his knees, and there is no body heat, and there is no movement in his chest. Maybe he's better this way; maybe he's more sanitary.

I touch my own face and my own hair. My hair is thin. My cheeks are flat. I have acne scars underneath my cheekbones. It is not enough. I have to feel all of myself, I have to know how I am any different from him. I rip my clothes off so my hands can feel. They wash board down my ribs, surf across my stomach where I can feel a pocket of fat beneath my belly button, two more on the top of my butt.

That night—that night he flicked the light on, and at first, it was like I was a diagram in a nursing textbook—all the ugly places got highlighted. My double chin. The pockets of fat that hugged my armpits, the fat flesh that cocooned my thighs, the burps of tissue on top of my hips. I feel them all now.

"Was it me?" I ask him as my hands creep down onto my knees—they bend in, like my mother's did. I know beneath me are my feet—the toes too long, and one of them curled in. "Did you look *at me*?" I ask him. I cup my breasts—the only small things on me, so small they are nearly flat. I hold them so tightly, they are turning red and they ache. I don't want him to see me now, but I am standing there naked in front of him. I fist my hands in his shirt because I don't want to touch myself anymore. I don't want to know any more about the way things are put together and held inside. Arm sockets and coils of intestines. Food goes in, shit comes out. "I told you to keep the light off. But you turned it on," I whisper, but it burns my throat just like a scream. My breath catches; I feel a sob climbing up my throat. I don't want to cry in front of him. I've already cried in front of him too many times. I point my finger at his face, but that is not enough. He did this to himself. He had to see me, and he did, and Selma said it. She was right. *If he saw you without your push-up on.* I open my hand; I slap him across the face hard, and there is enough life in him that it leaves a red mark, but it fades so quickly. Too quickly. I want marks on him. I want marks like the marks he left on my hips, the bruises at the flare of my waist. I want to feel it on my hand. I slap him again and again. I shove my finger into his chest. There is a tiny lamp beside him. I grab it and smash it on the table; I smash the dishes there. Their pieces fly everywhere, into his lap, into his hair, into my hands.

The shards cut me and remind of all the things he did to me, all the lies he told me. I curl my fists together, but it does not stop what is building inside of me. I clench my teeth together, but I can't hold anything back any more. My mouth won't stay shut. It's opening, it's opening, and I don't know what's going to come out. A sob or a scream or a noise like an animal. It's all of them.

In the morning, Selma still comes. She always comes. She finds me on the couch and nudges my shoulder and her face is sad.

"What did you do to yourself?" she asks. There are red marks all over me, and my body is still naked.

I tell her that this is all of me the way nobody wanted to see. She picks up a long lock of greasy hair from the floor. My scalp is light without it.

"No, babycakes. This isn't you. Not like this. I think I'll call someone now," Selma says.

"Okay?"

And it's funny that she is asking me okay because she isn't really asking me. She is telling me.

"I think I will close the house up, now," I say. "Just the way Dick is. I will close it all up tight, and I will stay inside."

"Oh, babycakes," says Selma. "If only that would help."

But it will. I know it will because it has worked for so long already. I will be a secret inside, and the house will keep me. •

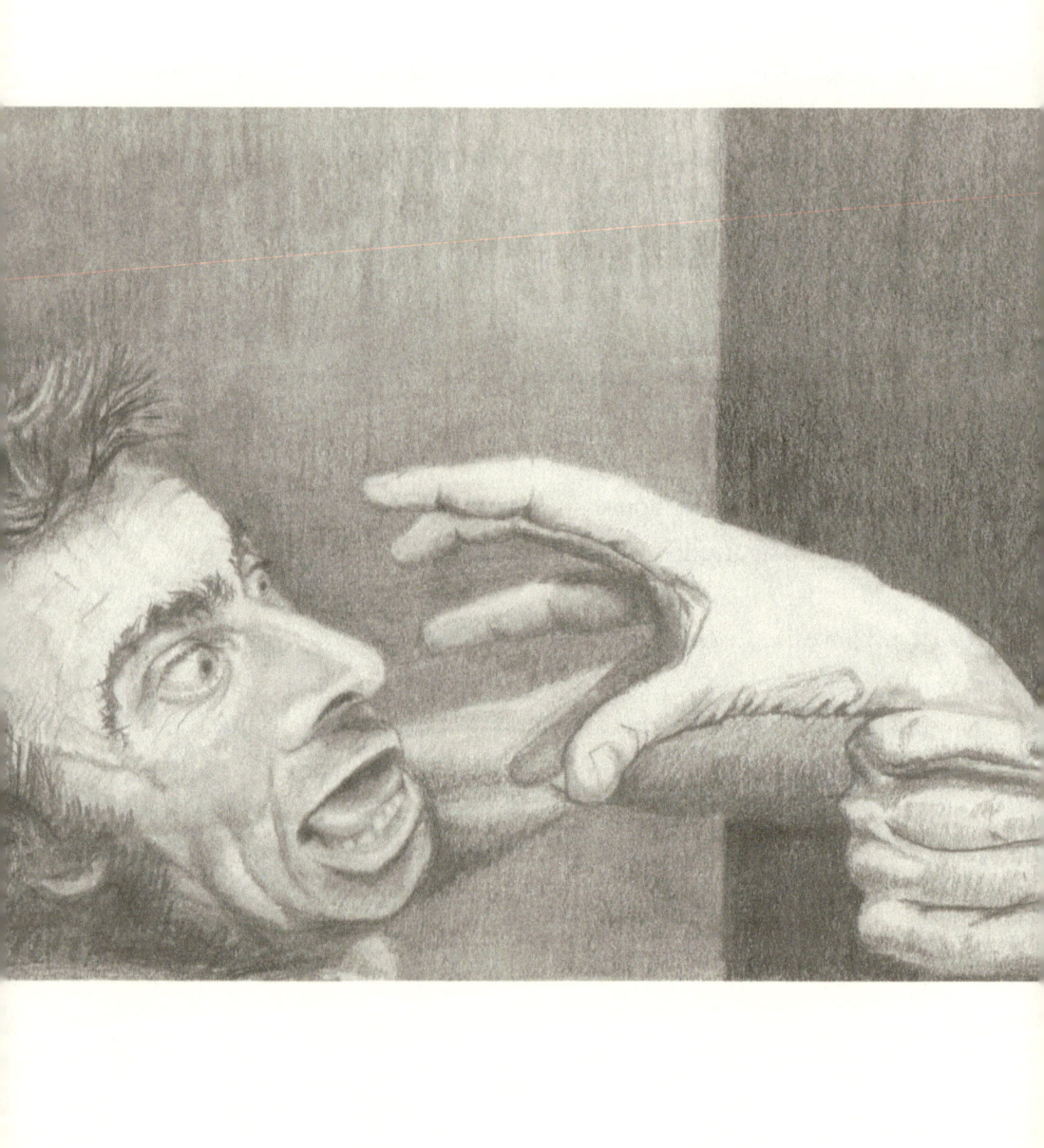

Self-Defence 2, Alisdair Small

Father is Proud

by Mathew Serback

"SON, I HAVE MUCH WISDOM TO GIVE YOU," MY FATHER SAID.

His teeth were made of tinfoil; his mouth always buzzed like a radio transmission whenever he opened it. The noise always distracted me when I was trying to talk to him. I'd follow the sound of the white noise from his mouth to my ears, losing whatever the meaning was in the translation.

The noise only got worse when he yelled. He and my mother would argue about the ways he used his leathery body on other women, and I would barely be able to make out the words he screamed over the thousands of locusts that were bursting out of his throat.

"That's your problem, son. You're never listening to me," my father said.

His face remained blank as he waited for a response. He didn't understand that I was trying to listen—that I was trying to respond, but I was distracted by the noise.

He couldn't hear the noise.

My father was not present when I was born; he didn't hear the news directly from the shaman and the healers. He never truly believed that I was born with water for blood. I knew it was real. I could feel the water sloshing around inside me at all times. Sometimes it even felt as if I was going to drown inside of my body.

"I'm sorry," I said to my father.

My father stood from his cobblestone throne with a torch in one hand, a bottle of whiskey in the other hand. When I was a baby he would feed me spoonfuls of whiskey; he claimed they were the lifeblood of the American man.

"Follow me," my father commanded.

He was headed for the dark. I didn't want to follow my father into the dark. I was terrified of the dark; my body felt heavier in the dark. I wasn't capable of moving as fast I wanted to escape the shadows. My father refused to acknowledge how difficult life was for me. To my father, moving through the dark was something that his father had taught him, something that he was merely handing down to me. To him there was no difference between walking in the dark and sinning—he was passing the knowledge—the lust—of them down to me.

I stumbled through the darkness. My body was a tire stuck in the mud, spinning in place as I labored after the light my father held. The torch in his hand bobbed in the dark before me, but continued to grow increasingly dimmer as it stretched out in the distance.

My father wasn't good at showing me patience.

"Father, I'm losing you," I yelled out into the dark as the light vanished out of the backdoor.

I waited for my father to call back to me, to hear that sound of cicadas to come calling for me, showing me the path, but it never came. I inched along in the dark, the water rolling from one side to the other, causing my body to rag doll from one wall in the dark to another.

I reached the door and pried it open with my hands. I was hit in the face by a burst of cold air, which was only matched by the trepidation I felt when I still didn't hear the banshee voice of my father calling out.

My father had not left or forgotten me; instead, he had lit torches along the path in the backyard for me to follow. The backyard was a sorted place. I followed along the torches I saw the shadows of the light fondling the smooth headstones of the graves that lined the yard.

When I was younger, I would look out the windows of our house and see people giving their bones to the Earth. My mother, with her tape-recorder-voice, would come and yell at me. She told me that there was nothing good about seeing the world *that* way: a world full of death.

My mother eventually climbed the beanstalk and went back into the sky to get cigarettes.

I had trouble maintaining my balance on the path; my momentum carried me in one direction as the path would curve, I would struggle to correct the motion of the ocean.

"Back here," my father's voice came echoing to me, "That's your problem son. You never learned to follow."

I ducked beneath a patch of overgrown brush. I saw my father standing there with the torch. He was right in front of the grain-shed where he stored his vats of booze. He stood next to the well we had in our backyard. The well had been our family's most prestigious gift that we passed along the lineage; it was the inheritance of fresh water.

I had only seen this part of our backyard once before; I had followed a snake out here. I stood for hours watching the snake move freely without a spine; it coiled and uncoiled and whispered the secrets of the sire to me. I was transfixed to its scales as it climbed the rotting blue fence that separated our lands. I sat down next to the snake and nuzzled my face against the chipped blue paint on the fence.

It felt like I was falling out of the sky – it felt like I was swimming in the sky.

"Your problem is you think too much," my father said.

My father poured some whiskey down the well.

I anticipated hearing the sound of the whiskey; I expected it to splash into the pool at the bottom, but there was nothing—no sound. I listened harder, with more intent. I was trying to hear the proof that there was a measurable depth to us.

There was still nothing.

Until there was something.

The screams that used to come from the neighbors houses and the graves were coming out of the well; there was the sound of children being beaten for their vehement denial of what their genes do to them. My mother told me, before she left, that children had to be beaten to keep order in the world.

"Father, I don't hear anything," I said.

"That's your problem. You never learned to suffer, son," my father said.

"I so desperately want to suffer for you father," I said, "I promise that I will stand here—I will not leave your side until I have heard all the sounds you need me to—until I've heard everything you have to say."

We stood—the sun rising and then hanging itself in the sky over and over again, solely for our amusement. For twenty years we stood in the backyard in almost complete silence. The only sound that I heard for twenty years was my father undoing the lid of the whiskey and pouring it into the mouth of the well.

"Father, it's been twenty years," I said, "There have been a million deaths of the sun and I still haven't heard a sound. I have given my entire life and I have nothing—not even your wisdom."

"I gave you everything you needed, son. What more could you have wanted than this?" My father asked.

"I wanted a life—to live, to love. I wanted to be more," I said.

"That's your problem. Everything you ever needed could be counted on one finger," my father said.

He pointed his index finger at me. I heard the cicadas crying out to me, but I didn't understand his words. I stuck my hand—wholly—into my mouth and used, what was left of my teeth that had rotted away from the long sips of whiskey, to bite clean through my fingers.

I pulled the fingers away and spat out jagged pieces of bone mixed with water onto the ground. I turned back to my father; my hand exposed to him, the thumb and index trickling faint traces of water before his eyes. The ring and pinky fingers wormed around in the dirt, dying a slow death in a pool of water next to my feet.

The only finger that was left was the middle one. It stood erect in the face of my father.

"Father, you have taught me everything you know," I said.

My father put down the bottle of whiskey and climbed on top of the stone that divorced us from the hole in the Earth. Bits of the stone broke apart beneath his weight. He looked through me; he looked out onto the paths that led us from home to here. He let out a primal yell—a yell that was full of fear—and let his body free fall into the well.

He was chasing after the whiskey and the twenty years of silence.

I waited to hear a sound – any sound.

Still, there was nothing. •

away and chase yersel!, Alisdair Small

A Conversation with Composer
Liew Niyomkarn

Editor Alexander Hogan interviews composer Liew Niyomkarn for The Flexible Persona *through a series of emails.*

LIEW NIYOMKARN IS A COMPOSER, sound artist, and electronics-lover from Bangkok, Thailand. She is interested in perception of sound, movement and texture. Liew currently resides in Los Angeles.

AH: I've really been enjoying your work over the last couple weeks. For some reason it's brought up in my mind the first time I heard an Ikue Mori CD. I remember getting into my car and listening to the CD from start to finish in the middle of a rainstorm. It made me really happy. I get that kind of feeling with your work, too. Kind of an expansion of perspective.

In a lot of your pieces repetition emerges, sometimes it's kind of soothing, sometimes it's even a little anxiety producing. Then the repetition settles in and as a listener I'm kind of caught in this place. Soothing or frenetic and then as I settle in, it dissolves and in a few seconds a new repetition/feeling emerges. It makes me wonder, how you feel in the performance, what's happening inside ...

LN: When I write my piece, I always think about telling stories, Sounds are invented, they merge to one another, they build a new identity and then they're shifting, breaking into smaller elements, they collapse. For me, this is a part of creating an adventure. I like to give people surprise, and I like to be surprised at the same time!

It is thrilling for me each time I do a solo performance because I don't usually practice my set that much. I do prepare my instrument and formulate composition, but when I'm in the situation where something that I cannot control, how much drinks an audience take, a temperature in a space, how many people in the show, for example, I pretty much allow myself to immerge in a present activity and play along with it. It makes me feel attentive and alert through my performance, as I have to be a listener and a performer at the same time.

AH: I like in-the-moment mindset. I notice, in the work of yours that's available to me, that there's a transition about three years ago. You were putting out some stringed pieces and though there are recognizable elements, I think of your more current work already present, it seems like a major shift. What led you from those acoustic and string works to your electronic work?

LN: My background is in music composition. My major instrument was classical guitar. After sophomore year, I found out I was stuck by limitation of the instrument. Meanwhile, my teacher introduced me to Pierre Schaeffer's *Etude aux objets* piece [https://www.youtube.com/watch?v=UQ7BZlV_ozQ], and I was amazed by it. I started to explore the technique he used in the piece; I started to do field recording, chopping and mixing sound sources and create a composition out of it. After I played around with this technique for a long time, I wanted to broaden more sound capabilities. It wasn't until in 2011 that I met my mentor, Mark Trayle. He introduced me to a programing language "Supercollider" (developed by James McCarthy), and I am totally hooked by its capability and versatility. I also studied SC with Scott Cazan. I was very lucky to have these two people show me what's available out there in the computer music world.

AH: It seems like a lot of your progression has been through removing limitations. Do you ever impose limitations on a piece or create problems you need to solve in your work?

LN: Interesting question!

I think before I create a piece, there's always some semi-strenuous factors there, an issue with a physical space or my piece is restrained to the bounded time of my designated performance, for example. I am not sure if it is called a problem? For me, I think it's more like a fun task. Maybe because I enjoy solving it I guess.

To answer your question about how I found my mentor: Actually, I studied with Mark Trayle while I was in Calarts. Simply to say that he didn't just give me artistic advice but also creative spirit, and that made a difference in my life in so many ways.

AH: Where do you see your work going in the future? What sounds and ideas are exciting to you now?

LN: I'm looking forward to carrying out more sound installation and sound sculpture. Besides, those two attempts, I am currently working on my instrument design, it will more or less look like nunchaku, a martial arts weapon, but opposite texture and functions. I have to make sure it won't hurt anyone and myself while I'm performing with it! (I'm insanely traveling to north of Thailand – to practice Kungfu for a week!)

Here is music I think is great and charming.

Starside - Bear Club – LA duo based, simply beautiful acoustic hippie band. [https://thebearclub.bandcamp.com/releases]

NODAL - Horacio Vaggione – Pioneer of micro sound. Feeling fresh every time I listen to this piece. [https://www.youtube.com/watch?v=th_Pqchfo3o]

Mare Imbrium - Sarah Davachi – Very beautiful drone music. [https://www.youtube.com/watch?v=oYVEomFRJfQ] •

BRODERICK MADDEN ARCHIVE

The Beast in the Jungle
Henry James

The Picture of Dorian Gray
Oscar Wilde

The Yellow Wallpaper
Charlotte Perkins Gilman

The Flexible Persona

What Remains of Mabel

by Sally Oliver

MABEL LIKED TO TOUCH THINGS, ANYTHING SHE COULD. SHE WAS ALWAYS tactile from birth. When I brought her out of my womb, I thought I felt her little hands tracing the scarlet passageway, feeling her way toward life. Blind and humiliated, she came out of me. She had been betrayed, shocked into existence. The high-pitched drone of human voices vied for attention; her first sight, her first signs of intimacy so warily bestowed in the bloody aftermath. I was silent when she cried and everyone surged forward to take her from me. I knew that she was still looking backward, that she would *always* be looking backward, for the incomparable warmth of that first compartment that preceded the delivery room. I had held her within a bloody chamber, close to death yet infinitely closer to life with every beat. The two possibilities twisted themselves into that fleshy rope from her belly to mine; she was blind to me yet she felt every tremor of my blood like a tide, which drew her closer to shore.

She lasted only five years beyond the delivery room. The funeral was thankfully short and I almost missed it. Not that I didn't show. I was present but I had vacated my body, left it on autopilot to absorb the stress and the sorrow of strangers while my consciousness was elsewhere. I actually had no memory of where I had been once I arrived home. I sat on the porch of the family home and considered that I had died for a brief period, perhaps four hours. I had eaten small tuna sandwiches shaped into little circles–Mabel always chose odd shapes for food–and I had drunk a little, not a lot, while people dutifully told me that they were sorry. My mother had said something about donating Mabel's clothes to a charity. Perhaps one for cancer? I had nodded and said nothing. I had just returned from the bathroom at this point, and I was paranoid that a small line of saliva had hardened around my mouth.

Gabriel was still clearing the plates away indoors. I was sitting on the porch with my head against the house as if I could prop it up, along with all the nameless dead signals that collected inside like dust. Inside was toxic; outside was best. Autumnal shades lent our backyard a beauty I had not noticed until now. All things clamored for occupancy in the periphery of my vision; the shed door loosened by the wind slammed upon itself time again and the cat from next door tore apart some live animal which was squabbling for release against the palate. Small wellington boots stood in line with an adult set by the shed door. Behind the static wall of my consciousness, a black spot had appeared. It swam along the blood and folded itself into the brain.

Gabriel called me from the house but I wanted him to come to me, I was becoming idle. He came to the porch and looked down at me with his glasses half covering the bottoms of his eyes. The pupils were lost.

"I've cleaned up in there. Not much else to do."

"Then for god's sake, sit down," I said.

He sat down beside me, and I felt a dim awareness of how handsome he was in white shirt and black tie. But I was tired, and dimly ashamed of being aroused.

"What are we going to do with her now?" I said.

Gabriel was unprepared for this. "What do you mean?"

"With Mabel?"

I thought of her ashes encased in a black box upstairs in our bedroom. I'd placed her on my pillow.

"Sarah, don't talk that way. Like she's still alive." Gabriel's voice had grown heavy.

"Her ashes then. What are we going to do about it?"

"We have so much time to worry about this." Gabriel took my arm because he thought touch was still relevant at this point. He touched me more now after Mabel's death than he ever did before. The negation of touch was enough to confirm to him in some painfully blatant manner that our marriage was defeated. I pulled away.

"I would prefer to send her off now so that she isn't just—" I had nothing.

Gabriel shifted his weight onto his left buttock closer to me. "Whatever happens now, the biggest part is over. We just saw it happen."

The biggest part is over. I thought of the little girl we'd brought into all this; five autumns of crushed leaves and catching worms under the nether regions of the hard earth. Little eyes too close together, nothing like her daddy and nothing like me. She'd gone somewhere we couldn't immediately follow. It wasn't like she'd turned down a supermarket aisle this time and I could drop the trolley and march down there after her, grabbing her by the waist by the groceries. One hard shiny apple in her little fist. This time she'd sloped forward into a space, an open void, of which I had no knowledge. To me, the notion that she'd preceded us into death produced a peculiar sensation in the back quarters of my lower body, my bowels perhaps. It was nausea. A terror so awesome it was like I had been undone to the last atom. On the first morning that she was dead, I'd had to pick up some milk for all ours had soured. The woman behind the shop counter had asked me, "Is that all?" *Is that all?* I couldn't rest with that question, prosaic enough at the time but indispensible to me now. Why bother at all? She'd gone first! Our Mabel: round, rosy-faced Mabel with the wandering hands. She had gone into the choppy waters of death alone, glittery black on the surface, which our minds could reach, but a myriad of uneven shades beneath. It was a solid flow of nothingness, stretching out daily, springing back in the night, winding round our lives now like an umbilical cord that hadn't been cut. Empty waters of aborted life. And I was carrying milk back to Gabriel for morning coffee. Where was she now? Was she looking in the face of God? Did she know where she was? Perhaps death was like a disused building full of gaudy corridors, designed for adults alone, and Mabel was wandering them alone. I had no one perspective of death. Sometimes I had none and was convinced that she was purely nothing.

"We'll think of something," said Gabriel.

*

In the end we decided to travel to my sister's house in Carson City. Georgia had invited us to visit the moment Mabel had died; she was insistent that we come and stay for as long as we liked and, since I was a freelance writer and had taken leave on account of Mabel's illness, I was free to distract myself in whichever way I could. I knew instinctively that Georgia saw this as a way of making amends for her absence at the funeral. She rarely travelled to see us in Sacramento, preferring instead to rely upon others to come to her.

She lived with her husband, Terence, in their large house full of New Age stones, crystals and incense sticks burning slowly in the house like sacred, spindly cigars. She was quixotic and generally opened her mind to almost anything that she believed flattered her primal unconscious desires. Often she liked to discuss this 'unconscious' undercurrent that dictated her actions and ideologies, her interest in the environment and its healing agency, always at great length and with a certain premeditated and slightly self-conscious quality in her words. It was as though she believed she saw the flow of her unconscious with her own eyes, contrary to Freud's insistence that it was forever unknowable, invisible to the ego like God himself. Georgia had already made contact. She lay beside the river to see which direction it flowed, caressing the wrinkled surface with her fingers. Apparently, nobody else had ventured deep enough but herself. Her discussions on *surfaces* were interminable. She loved bringing new people into her home so that she could probe new surfaces. Her psychoanalyses were unflinching and often made people wary of revealing too much of themselves to her. *There is always another surface beyond the last one*, she liked to say, *no matter how close you come to your center, there is always some other fence to jump, some other wall to give way. The very last surface is always the one, which sits on top of death.*

I suspected that she invited us out of her own desire for novelty, for a different charge in the electric current of the house with the addition of newer voices, newer emotional crises to shift the old ones away from the core. Stagnation was a problem she also could not easily escape, and I sometimes suspected that she would go mad if she didn't always have a new set of guests to stay with her and Terence, and new neuroses to play with. But now I didn't care what her motive in inviting us. More than anything, I wanted to get moving from my pain. I had become a prisoner to every dead impulse in my body. It took more energy than it was worth to do anything at all, to lift my head from sleep and check the alarm clock; to fall back again, defeated by four red digits suspended on the void. Ennui places a harness on the heart. With every hour it tightens and pulls as though to bring it back in line with hope, then grows slack when hope dies in the next breath. This was my last hope: to get moving, to get on the road and to take Mabel with us.

Gabriel drove and I sat with her on my knee. She was the last possession

I took from the house when we packed the car, her ashes resting in a black enameled chest the size of a lunchbox. I wanted her to sit with us in the front of the car as Gabriel drove the rocky track through Eldorado Forest. We were going to cast her ashes on the way to Georgia. We would visit Lake Tahoe, which was close to where Georgia lived, and we would sail out upon the lucid blue water to give Mabel her final resting place. It seemed a perfect plan. We had taken her there last year after all and she was happy. We were happy. The photograph on the mantelpiece told us that we were happy. What more validation was there of this than the frank objectivity of a camera lens? It is immemorial proof of a 'family outing'. Water lapping the sailboat, mountainous surroundings and heat that remains forever palpable in print. A sunny child, patient child, her mother holding the hat on her head to keep the wind from stripping her scalp bare. The woman squints and allegedly she is smiling, though I wonder whether I will ever be able to believe it.

"I've missed this track," said Gabriel out of the blue. We were passing through the Eldorado Forest. I watched out of the window for deer, wondering what would happen if one was to step boldly into the road at the last minute. I craved diversion in all its forms.

"Do you think Mabel would like what we're doing?" I said.

Gabriel's mouth stiffened, and he drew his eyes to the rear mirror.

"It's what you want to do. That's why we're doing it."

"Yes, but I want to think Mabel would like it too," I said needlessly.

"Sarah. It doesn't matter that way. The remains of the dead are for the comfort of the living. This is for our benefit."

"It comforts *me* to know that she would have liked it." I felt myself turning on him already and we had barely left the main road. "You're saying you don't care whether Mabel would be happy with what we're doing?"

"I'm saying she won't ever know what we do for her now. If you want to bury her or send her off in the wind it doesn't matter to her now. She's not going to see it happen is she?"

"State the obvious why don't you."

The muscle in Gabriel's neck grew taut. He looked directly at me, which he knew I didn't like when he was driving.

"Watch the road Gabriel."

"What are you sniping at me for anyhow? It's like I can't ever grieve for her in the specific way you want."

A car sounded his horn at us in passing. Gabriel had veered slightly into the middle of the road.

"You wouldn't even speak about her at the funeral. What, did you have absolutely nothing to say? Keep your damn eyes on the road!"

He looked away from me and his face emptied itself abruptly. I had hurt him but he needed to be hurt. I needed to know he felt the same annihilation in his body like I did. Otherwise I was alone.

"Why didn't you say anything?" I pushed it.

"I had nothing I wanted to say to all those people," he said darkly. "Mabel knew how I felt about her. Why do I have to declare it over and over to people who need to make a spectacle of it?" He lost his voice a bit, found it again as we rounded a campsite. A child ran forward to see us behind the sunny windscreen. "Talking does nothing. Nor does singing, praying, chanting-whatever. Even what we're doing now, it's just an empty symbol of releasing her somewhere of our choosing. It affects nothing but our own consciousness of her. Her own is over. We don't contain it."

I hated him without reserve then. I hated him beyond anything else; any other apprehension of him was swallowed up in that tide. Its quality was as fluid in motion as love. It kept coming forward, retreating every now and again in disbelief, then creeping forward again to claim the memory that had moved it. I sat in silence for the rest of the journey.

*

When we arrived at Lake Tahoe, in spite of my dull spirits, I felt a familiar pull toward its iridescent waters. The heat, colossal beyond the shore, was abruptly broken up by the cool surface of a striking blue, a commanding blue. Its color was hostile to vague and dim realities, the ultimate contradistinction of all surfaces that sought to drain the mind of hope. There I felt the clarity of life, assured that it would take anything into its depths—my foot, my hand, the tips of my fingers—as though it was sacred.

After parking the car, we followed the track to the boathouse. I carried Mabel in her box under my fleece, already regretting her loss. Second loss to the first. Gabriel eyed the square-shaped lump pressed against my stomach and frowned in thought. He asked to hire a sailboat for an hour and the young man smiled obligingly before he gave us both lifejackets. He was surprised by the little black box I was unwilling to part with as we stepped into the boat but he nodded quaintly as though he understood something though what it was I had no clue. I was not dying to know. Other people's perceptions of us had ceased to annoy me since Mabel's passing.

The man continued to initiate us into the business of sailing, managing the main sail, the tiller and so on. Gabriel cut him off abruptly.

"We've sailed before, not so long ago. We can manage, thank you."

"Sure, sure. Well you enjoy yourselves!" he said and gave the boat a smart push. I settled myself close to the port and rested Mabel on my knee. The boat rocked slightly as we left the pier and we were suddenly competing with other families all jostling for space on the water, parents directing children to sit tight, couples laughing and trying to take the perfect spontaneous photograph, teenagers attempting to knock one another out with the boom. Gabriel placed his hand on the mainsheet. I placed mine on the box that held Mabel.

"Whereabouts do you want to do it?" he said.

It was a bizarre thought amidst all this communal good cheer. I felt, for the first time, the irreconcilability of what we had previously discussed to do and its actual physical reality, here among so much life and noise that was impersonal to me. Our quest was both morbid and ridiculous.

"I don't know, just keep moving until we're further out."

"No definite spot?"

"No, not really."

Mabel liked to touch things, always had. I saw her a year ago touching the water here as though it told her something we never had. Her plump fingers brushed the surface, and I watched her eyes narrow with her smile. Eyes ever so slightly too close together but sweet in nature. They weren't large or far-reaching, they did not indicate a sharpness of insight or intelligence, but they were considerate, precociously considerate for her age. That was why I believed she was so tactile, it was not her desire to feel but her desire to touch everything she felt right to the core and change it in some way so that it was better, less troubled and defeated. She touched me often without need but with love. Simple, non-insistent love. I would try to keep hold of the physical memory of her compact form burying itself into the hollow space of my body. She wanted to warm me through because she sensed the stern quality of grief, the apprehension of death that we had carried from the hospital and allowed to linger around her last days. I, who had been so occupied with keeping that damned hat on her head so people wouldn't notice her illness, I, who had argued with Gabriel about the mainsail flapping too much, who had cried a little when we'd forgotten to bring a packed lunch with us in the car. Miserable mother! Miserable wife!

Once we had sailed out a fair distance from the shore, Gabriel lowered the sail and the boat glided aimlessly adrift. He shifted his glasses far back across the ridge of his nose and watched me.

"You think this is a good spot then?" I said.

"Sure. It's as good as any."

I opened the lid and looked inside. Grey dust, soft as sand, hugged the sides of the box. When I titled the whole thing, it slid easily as one mass. I poked the grainy texture with my finger and left a small crater in its surface.

What would Mabel have done? A strange thought. It was an image I had grappled with in sleep for the past few weeks, or rather a series of images. Perhaps from watching Mabel play with glitter and glue at the kitchen table, I imagined her doing the same with her ashes, casting them in the air like confetti, blowing them across an infinite wooden surface. Or perhaps she would have buried them into the earth like she did with her seeds in the garden, patting the soil down with her palms enough times to bring the worms to the surface. She appeared every night with some new desire to impart to me, touching everything indiscriminately. Her remains fell through the stream of my consciousness, transforming every second into something beyond death. What lay in that little black box was something much less but also something infinitely more than dull remains. It was her little hands reduced to dust. It was also what the universe had spared from total nothingness at the last minute.

"I don't want to," I said.

Gabriel lifted his hand to wipe the sweat from his forehead.

"Why not?" he said.

"I changed my mind. Let's go back." I closed the box but Gabriel was wary of my change of heart and mistrusted it.

"I thought this was what you wanted. Why don't you want to do it?"

"It's too sad."

Gabriel bent his head. He looked exhausted.

"I want to keep her. Or do something else instead but not this," I said. I was irritated by myself too; I didn't blame him for that. "I can't stand the thought of throwing her overboard like this, it's too sad."

"Of course it's fucking sad," Gabriel snapped. "It *was* sad, it *is* sad, it will *always* be fucking sad. She died—that is the sad part! You have to stop finding new ways to relive it, new ways to lose hold of her! It has happened. We lived it. This—" He gestured to the box, the water. "—is not going to change anything."

"Stop talking to me like that," I said. "God knows you've said that enough! *It doesn't mean anything.* What does then? Or do we just forget her like she never happened?" I held the box tightly. "You know, Gabriel—" My voice grew thin, and I was afraid I'd lose it. "We don't remember everything. Nobody does! I'm already frightened I can't remember every part of her face and everything she said, all her words. It's worse, *worse* than what you're saying. She is still alive, just, in my mind and she's dying every day there!"

We said nothing and the boat rocked. Gabriel's eyes were watery, but I couldn't tell whether it was just from sheer exhaustion. Or perhaps grief for some people is purely a form of exhaustion. For me it is continually being pushed over the edge into ever-mounting waves of hysteria. Now I am the child. He is the weary patriarch. I no longer felt anything between us that resembled an adult relationship.

"You won't change your mind," he said flatly.

"No."

He rested against the side of the boat for a moment. Then I saw a small spasm break up the rest in his body; his back and arms shuddered as it passed through. Sharp as a contraction. He stood up and adjusted the sail.

As we moved back along the tide toward our starting point, I wondered what was to be done with Mabel. Were we to admit defeat and keep her in her little coffin, forever gathering dust on top of dust? Some people keep ashes in jars on top of mantelpieces like totem poles, a trite gesture of their prominence within the domestic space. It seemed so grotesque to my mind. And Mabel could never be an ornament, paralyzed into receiving every piece of conversation, every dead sigh beyond the living room. Gabriel had agreed. "We're not Victorians," he had said, "I'm not keeping human remains in the house." It wasn't just that it was morbid; it would instantly incriminate every other principle activity that took place immediately beyond it. How could we watch comedy re-runs on TV or eat takeout while Mabel's ashes lay somewhere in the house? She would transform every prosaic action into something hideously profane. I would never be able to strip naked with the knowledge that my child lay in brittle pieces in the next room. But then where lay the divide? What is to be done to cure the visceral longing, as well as the nausea, that death leaves in its wake? My desire to touch Mabel was measured only by my guilty need to have done with what remained of her. One day it was her. The next day it was something else, something other, and I shuddered.

I no longer knew how to think of her. I only knew that my want of her was a living thing that grew in the lining of my stomach and brain. There would be no relief and I didn't want it.

*

Gabriel and I didn't speak for the rest of the journey to Carson City. In spite of everything, I was glad when we arrived there. It is the kind of arid, mountainous landscape that is just bleak enough for comfort. To be enclosed within a desert terrain just beyond the immediate tower blocks of the city was reassuring in some primordial way. Georgia and Terrence lived on the outskirts of the city in a renovated Victorian house, which commanded no great view from the front but plenty of beauty from behind. When we strolled up the driveway, I saw her already waiting for us in the doorway. She was wearing a long white cotton dress that looked like it was a relic from the seventies, and her dark hair was hanging in loose waves down to her waist. Her eyes were unfocused as always, the pupils darting everywhere at once as if to take her full share of the universe before she turned her back on it. She wore nothing on her feet but proceeded to step outside all the same.

"Hi, Sarah," she charged forward and began to open car doors, taking our bags at random. "I'm so glad you're here. I've been very ill." She reached forward to take my bag, and I heard her voice deep in the recesses of the boot. "So sorry I couldn't come to the funeral."

Gabriel shared an irate expression with me before she ducked back up again.

"How are you doing though, seriously?" She moved close to me and spoke to all my features in turn; my eyes, my nose, my mouth, my collarbone. "I want you to talk to me about everything. Tell me about Mom. Was she there? I haven't forgiven her yet for what she said to me last time she was here."

"What was that?" I said. I was quick to take Mabel's box from the passenger seat before she found it.

"Oh, just the usual about having a kid: *You're thirty three now, Georgia! It'll be harder to be a mother the longer you leave it!* I mean—" she stumbled and dropped my bag for a moment, turning to me. "—has it crossed her mind that I might actually enjoy not being a mother? I have no deep-seated maternal instinct beyond the surface that satisfies her. God knows, I know—" She picked up the bag to head in but dropped it again to face me. "I know how awful it is that she hasn't any grandchildren now, that *you* haven't a child anymore, but I can't be expected to fill the void!"

"Jesus, Georgia, we've only just got here," said Gabriel.

Once we were inside she dropped our bags by the stairway. Their house was enormous, but Georgia had still managed to make it look entirely cluttered. She never seemed to clean often and she was scatty about storing things, often placing everything where she felt it ought to be with her mood at the time. She told us she'd take our things up later and took us through to the kitchen. I could smell something like burnt sage.

"Terence is outside," said Georgia. She leaned through the window. "They're here Terence. Get your skinny ass in here!" She smiled when she turned to us. "So, you want some coffee?"

When Terence entered, I saw the source of the smell. He had been smoking weed in the back yard. Tall and thin like a gangly teenager, he sloped indoors and rested the joint on the kitchen counter.

"Hey, Sarah, Gabriel. Come here." He embraced us. "So sorry for you both." He drew back. He always had this hangdog look, a desolate but at the same time humorous aspect to his face which was dark-skinned, a little grubby. He took my hand again and pressed his thumb in the palm. "You can stay here as long as you want. Before we drive you crazy!"

Georgia smiled indulgently and looped her arms around his neck.

"I was just telling Sarah about what Mom said last time she was here," she murmured into his neck. "She's becoming unbearable."

I could feel Gabriel straining himself into a knot beside me, the tendons running tight beneath the skin.

"I mean, why should I have to justify my life to her? It's like she's breathing down my neck every time she's here! She's too much. And so emotionally *stunted*. I mean, I can see why she hates coming here. She hates that I'm living the life I want and she obviously never had."

She started looking for coffee cups, shifting boxes of cereal and empty milk bottles on the counter. When she stood on tiptoe to reach the cupboards I saw that the soles of her feet were an ashy grey.

"She talks with a hard mouth now, have you noticed that?" She gave up looking for the cups and took the kettle instead. "Her mouth is receding. I think it's the first sign of a dried up sex life—a hard, thin mouth. The lips gone inward."

"Georgia, stop," I said.

"Sorry, but it's true. And she's using us, well—" She looked at me with exaggerated regret. "—using *me*, as a surrogate for rearing children so that she can still feel, I don't know—" She paused and abandoned the kettle, staring into space now. "—connected to *new life* again. Connected to something that sees the world innocently."

"Which is what we're all striving for," said Terence.

"Hey, Sarah, we had this brilliant idea," said Georgia suddenly. She clawed at my arm. "We're going to light a bonfire tonight. You've never come to see us in the fall after all and it's going to be a musky night, I can feel it in my bones."

Her eyes narrowed and I recognized something in their expression that vaguely troubled me somewhere beyond my consciousness. An unexpected association with something else, faintly melancholy like the print of a hand on a frosted window. The recognition was too quick and slipped under the tissue of my thoughts as fast as Georgia's face changed its expression.

"Nice idea," I said. I looked at Gabriel who had barely spoken since we arrived. "Georgia, do you mind if we take our things upstairs? I need a lie down."

"Sure. You have a sleep. I'm so glad you're here," she said and threw her arms around me. For a moment I felt, for the first time since Mabel's death, the pleasure of touching another body. I was surprised by real unaffected warmth from her and gave way to it.

Once Gabriel and I were in the guest room, I sat on the end of the bed and surveyed everything. Georgia had featured the room with prints of surreal and gothic paintings by Lucas Kandl, Francis Bacon and Raymond Douillet. I stared at images of naked breasts, flanks and faces that lay suspended on a backdrop of darkness or scarlet blood-red.

"She doesn't mean to be tactless," I said.

Gabriel straightened up from unpacking our clothes. His arms hung on the air as though he was tired of them. He looked as though he no longer wanted ownership of his body and would lease it out to anyone who wanted it. He no longer lived in it now; he simply tolerated it. Sometimes I might catch him staring at his limbs as though he had forgotten what they were for. I wanted him more in these moments than when he was purveying his options in the physical world, looking for refuge in work, food and sleep, like nothing had happened; a prosaic soldier of reality.

This made me despair beyond what sheer emptiness could do. I moved closer to the space between his thighs and placed my hands on them.

"She doesn't mean to, but she does anyway and it's the same fucking difference to me," he said. "She's egocentric. Always will be probably. It couldn't take a death in the family to shift the center of her consciousness."

"She's still trying to help. In her own way. She's letting us stay after all."

"You saw the way she launched herself at us as soon as we arrived," said Gabriel. His mouth was hard and empty. "She propels herself at people. That's what she does. She coaxes people in and then shuts off all emotional inquiry. We all orbit her shallow little life for a brief while and she retains this gravitational pull for as long as she needs to feel safe until she throws us off again." He kicked the bed sharply and I pulled my feet up. "She is more cruel than you'll ever admit."

"Gabriel, don't be angry."

"Why not?" He began to pace the room, his arms trailing after him. "She is everything I hate in a woman. Self-centered, self-appraising. And cruel without realizing it. I mean, take these pictures for example."

He rested his eyes on a particular print by Douillet. It depicted a procession of human figures walking out of the womb of a woman with the flesh come away from her skull. They began to grow from infants into children and then adolescents, adults, seniors, sauntering a desert path toward the womb of another woman. This last woman was made of stone. By the end of the line, the newborn had withered into a husk of a creature, stooping low to enter the tomb-like parting of her legs.

"That's just her taste," I said.

"You don't think she's provoking us by hanging these in here?"

"No, I really don't."

"You're a fool."

He relented then, as though he was too weary to continue or he thought he had gone too far. He wandered back to me and sat by my side. For a few seconds he remained impervious to everything but once I placed my hand on his thigh he surprised me by the suddenness in which he seized it.

"Let's go back home," he said.

I sensed a physical collapse in him; he was searching for some of my former tenderness. It had been a year, perhaps longer, since I'd let him make love to me. His need was always there, hanging mournfully around the house, pressing onto my shoulders as I made coffee, chasing my ankles when I walked up the stairs. But I could not allow myself to walk both worlds while Mabel was sick and dying. My womb weighed heavy for the little girl who was about to leave me and step into a place beyond what I could see. Annihilation settled like a film of dust in my body. The space between that first tug of my uterus and the last nail of the coffin was closing up. Had I space for Gabriel there? I admit I actually resented that he thought so. Instead I turned my body to Mabel, reserved its last ebb of intimacy for her. Gabriel's lust muddled things, made everything much sadder to bear and harder to negotiate. Besides, it was not a kind of lust that I was familiar with. Gabriel looked for me in the house to fend off his own affiliation with death, to seek new comfort in the flesh of a mother as opposed to a wife. He had never before wanted to sleep with his chin resting between my breasts or his face pressed into my crotch but that was where I found it some nights. We both recognized a new level of abject despair in his advances that made us cringe, I for his sake.

Now I knew I was the agent to restore that old rope of love, tie it back together before it wound up on another side of the universe. But my hands were heavy and the rope was too. But I knew he was becoming bitter, acerbic, short-tempered. The mask was slipping and a new face was emerging. I had first sight of it at the funeral. I had seen it the night of Mabel's death when I wanted to sleep in another room, away from him. Was I cruel? I might have been but I couldn't sleep with the last memory of Mabel and Gabriel's hangdog lust in the same room. I dreaded the god awful collision of lust and death, lust created through death: frightened, frantic lust that demanded every inch of me! Nausea had closed me up for the night and I sank away from his body, resigned myself to the room next door.

Now he plucked my hands open and folded his inside.

"Will you come back with me?" said Gabriel.

"We can't go back now."

"Hey, we're gonna light the fire!" Georgia called upstairs. "Sun's going down!"

*

Once the sun had set over the Nevada desert the fire began to gather pace, contributing its own measure of beauty to the blank sky. Stretch upon stretch of stars were coming forward, wreathed in smoke and shimmying from side to side. As we sat beneath them I held Gabriel's arm like a prop to keep me safe from the creeping emptiness at the corners of our great light. The fire burned on as Georgia threw an assortment of bizarre items on there: ornaments, clothes, a registration plate, an old guitar. Terence helped her at first but eventually grew bored and crouched by the bottom, muzzling his face behind his jacket collar.

"We need more fuel for it," said Georgia, finally squatting next to us. "I have some herbs that I can burn in the house."

"What would they do exactly?" said Gabriel witheringly.

"I thought of putting some thyme on there. Thyme is a purifying incense, which I burn in the house a lot; it's supposed to increase psychic awareness. Say, do you have anything you'd like to burn?"

"Like what?" I said.

"Anything you want to expunge from your life? Something that's clogging it up at the core?"

"I have nothing," I said.

Georgia faced the fire and her face was illuminated by a dozen colors, some of them bringing out parts of her face I had never seen before.

"I have some yarrow flower too. That's good for melancholy, depression, ennui. It brings you back round to your true unconscious self while stripping it of all those things which cage it on a daily basis."

Gabriel snorted angrily. He no longer had the patience to humor her.

"Get whatever you want and put it on there," I said. I was growing languid and the heat had a scorching effect on my patience too. Though I was kinder than Gabriel, I had no impulse left for anger, only despair. And that was stretching itself beside me now on the grass, across the stars and into the desert, free at last to roam and gnaw itself to death. I thought of Mabel's ashes in our room, lying on the bed. Everything revolved around it.

Georgia got up and headed back in the house to find her herbs. For a short moment we three watched one another across the flames and forgot to smile.

"It's a real sad thing, your Mabel dying," said Terence shyly. His eyes were black after watching such a great light and I wondered whether mine were too.

"Yes, it's sad," said Gabriel. His body alone gave the required response but there was nothing left of him in the words.

When Georgia came back she was carrying an armful of little packets with herbs and powders inside. We watched as she shook them out, musty herbs and plants like the ones we used to seal in the pages of flower pressing books. It was a strange event: the three of us watching her, too sad or stoned to give way to her enthusiasm. For it took over the night and asked for all the elements to appraise it. She bounced up and down on her bare feet, her breasts half toppling out of her white dress. It was then that I recognized the expression I'd seen before which had troubled me. Her eyes, brightened by the fire, were like Mabel's though they were less defenseless. It had taken me five years to see the resemblance.

Eventually Gabriel decided to head back into the house. Terence lay slumped against the foot of a tree now, his legs in line with the roots. Only Georgia and I remained with the fire. Her energy hadn't faltered one moment; in fact I believe she grew more expansive with the heat. I sat further back now, the fire was biting my face and I began to wander in spirit to the bed where Gabriel had taken himself.

Georgia still had more to give to the fire. I had begun to drift off when she came back again with another treasure from the house and this time she carried it more carefully than before. It looked like a small black box yet I couldn't be sure; my eyes were hot and a thick mist lay in my retinas through which everything seemed to have bled into the red spot at the center. Sometimes I opened my eyes and Georgia was miles from it, then when I was about to close them she had merged into it like all things. Then I saw her open the box and I sat up to watch. Without any prelude, I saw her cast the contents in the fire. She scooped everything out with her hands as though it was sand on the beach, willfully scattering it everywhere. She tossed up the little clouds of dust so that they fell in as many places as she could find for them in the flames.

The blood reeled back and I felt the shock of her loss again, like a tight black hole in my brain. I was appalled and relieved. I couldn't have prepared myself for what she did yet I couldn't help but rejoice in the cruelty of it, for it had spared me from a cruel decision. By taking things into her own hands, she performed the exorcism I was unwilling to do of my own will. The mother in me sank down in horror on her knees, but a second self broke the membrane, stepped back into the world for another go at life. Georgia tipped the box, emptying the last of Mabel into the fire and her ashes were now finally intermingled with everything else. She was intangible, finally, in every sense of the word and I would no longer be tricked into believing otherwise.

When she had finished, Georgia came and sat next to me. She said nothing but she took my arm.

"How did you know that was her?" I said.

"I guessed as much. You said you were going to take her to Lake Tahoe, then I saw the box on your bed and I knew you hadn't done it." She turned her eyes on me, which were black from watching the fire. "You don't mind?"

I paused before answering.

"Too late to mind now. She died after all didn't she?"

Besides, I was tired. It may have seemed cruel of me, but I was also too tired to care about that too. I would attend to Mabel again but surely I was justified in occasionally seeking refuge from her? The waves always came rolling back, but for now I was standing somewhere south of their border with my ankles dry. This side was reserved for my ascent back into life. I anticipated falling back on myself every single day while the sand returned to sludge at the break of another wave. I turned and Mabel would be there with her feet at the bottom and her face just resting on the surface, bobbing up and down. The question was always whether to join her.

After the fire burned to nothing, I went out to see the remains of it that morning. There was a thick scent of wood and herbs that clotted the air, and I reached out to touch the ashes. Georgia grew wild flowers in the back yard and I plucked their heads, one by one, and scattered them on what remained of the fire and my child. They fluttered briefly in their arc before resting at my feet. •

Contributors | Spring 2016

Elena Botts

Elena grew up in the D.C. area, lived briefly in Berlin and Johannesburg, and now attends college in upstate New York. She's been published in fifty literary magazines over the past few years. She is the winner of four poetry contests, including Word Works Young Poets Competition. Her poetry has been exhibited at the Greater Reston Art Center and at Arterie Fine Art Gallery. Check out her poetry books, *we'll beachcomb for their broken bones* (Red Ochre Press, 2014), *a little luminescence* (Allbook-Books, 2011) and *the reason for rain* (Coffeetown Press, expected publication in fall 2015). Her visual art has won her several awards. Go to elenabotts.com and o-mourning-dove.tumblr.com to see her latest work.

Gael DeRoane

Gael DeRoane is a tennis coach based in Pennsylvania. His work has appeared in *London Journal of Fiction*, *Page & Spine*, *Rose Red Review*, *Opiate*, *Clockwise Cat*, *Punchnel's*, and *Fiction on the Web*. He invites anyone who likes arthropods to read *Arvin the Discontented Spider*, available at Amazon in e-book format.

Cris Harris

Cris Harris teaches writing and experiential education at an independent school outside of Cleveland, OH. His essays and poems have appeared recently at *The Flexible Persona*, *Alice Blue Review*, *Skylark Review*, *New South* and *Rogue Agent*.

Henry Marchand

A shy, retiring creature at home in the forests and dunes of California's central coast, Henry Marchand also frequents the campus of Monterey Peninsula College, where he teaches and coordinates the Creative Writing program. His fiction and nonfiction have appeared in *Cleaver Magazine*, *The Seattle Review*, *Review Americana*, *Elysian Fields Quarterly*, *Rosebud*, *The New York Times*, *The International Herald-Tribune* and elsewhere. He has written a screenplay about the dangers of messing with the DNA of feral hogs and is writing a novel with no hogs in it at all, so far. Asked about the ongoing success of the San Francisco Giants he will answer, "Bochy and Rags." He is adamant that "every day" must be retained as the adverbial form and that the Great American Novel has already been written, so everyone should really just move on and relax already.

K. L. Morris

K. L. Morris earned her M.F.A. from Lesley University. Her work has appeared in *Body Parts Magazine: A Journal of Horror and Erotica*. She spends most of her time writing, walking her dog, and ignoring her husband in order to write. When no one's around, she writes inside of a tent with a large glass of wine. When people are around, she writes inside of a tent with a large glass of wine and the door zipped shut. She's neither as broody nor as introspective as she presents herself. Connect with her on Twitter @KareMoreIs. She blogs (infrequently) at www.thewritinggeek.com.

Liew Niyomkarn

Liew Niyomkarn is a composer, sound artist, and electronics-lover from Bangkok Thailand. She is interested in perception of sound, movement and texture. Liew currently resides in Los Angeles.
http://www.liewniyomkarn.com

Sally Oliver

Sally's stories have been published in *The Blueshift Journal*, *Riding Light Review*, *94 Creations*, *The Flexible Persona* and an anthology of short fiction titled *Fugue II* by The Siren Press. She works as a Sales and Marketing Assistant for W W Norton Ltd in London and studied English Literature at Lancaster University where she received a 1st BA and MA with Distinction. Sally is currently writing her first novel, a modern tragedy which echoes man's original sin, inspired by the Pink Floyd album Animals.

Heather Parry

Heather is a ghostwriter, editor and fiction writer currently based in Edinburgh. After completing a B.A. in English Literature and Philosophy from the University of Manchester, she lived around the world for 6 years learning how to properly tell a tale, and was part of a live storytelling project in Panama City, Panama. She likes to write about impossible things, as well as about utopias, dystopias and real life, which is somewhere in between.

You can find out more about Heather at her website, heatherparry.com.

Mathew Serback

Mathew Serback is twenty eight years old. Honestly, he had to check with someone to verify he was correct. He can moonwalk on a treadmill (if it's set at the correct speed for moonwalking). He hosts a podcast called *Nation of Bootleggers*; sometimes he talks to himself and sometimes he is talking to himself while ignoring other people in the conversation. You can find his work in *Scissors & Spackle*, *Repurposed Magazine*, *On the Rusk*, and other publications.

Alisdair Small

Based in Glasgow, Scotland, 37-year-old human Alisdair Small struggles to draw and paint his ever-evolving view on himself, reality and the world. His process is non-logical where walking taking photographs, engaging with nature, skateboarding, dreaming and doodling eventually lead to finished work.

The works that are on display in the Spring 2016 issue are "self-defence," which is a humorous take on the issue of self confidence, putting yourself down or holding yourself back. They are both self portraits and are drawn with penicil on paper. Next up is "away and chase yersel!," which is drawn with pen and ink on paper. This piece is again a self portrait, this time of the artist chasing himself. The image has been based on the slang term that the piece is named after. It's a term used in annoyance of someone bothering someone such as a child or a friend, and it just means go and find some one else to annoy.

You can find more of Alisdair's work @facebook.com/AllySmallartwork, @instagram skateboarding_sheep, artwanted.com/alisdairsmall.

www.ingramcontent.com/pod-product-compliance
Lightning Source LLC
Chambersburg PA
CBHW021925170626
46807CB00007B/2986